**Now I h~~ave read~~ Frances Weaver
and I no longer want to be young again.
What a marvelous companion for
these next, golden, years!**

Howard Rayfiel
Paramount Pictures

Golden Roamers

— it's a wild and warm
and wonderful romp
by a fine writer.

Barnaby Conrad

Director
Santa Barbara (California) Writer's Conference

To Bonnie
Christmas 1994

Mariette

GOLDEN ROAMERS

THE UNPUBLISHED JOURNAL
OF LILLIAN MORRISON

Frances Weaver

*With incidental drawings
from the author's sketchbook*

Cover illustrations by Roger Roth

MIDLIFE MUSINGS

Saratoga Springs
New York

1992

ISBN 0-9617930-5-8

Cover design
Melanie Wegner
Alstrom / Peña Creative Services
Albuquerque, New Mexico

Book design, editing and production
Wallace W. Abbey
Piñon Consulting
Pueblo, Colorado

Printed in the United States of America

10 9 8 7 6 5 4 3 2 1

Published by
Midlife Musings
P. O. Box 970
Saratoga Springs, New York 12866

LILLIAN MORRISON . . .

never rode on this bus. Not the real Lillian Morrison. As far as I know, Lillian Morrison never played shuffleboard, either. I have no doubts, however, that Lillian Morrison's lifestyle and her adventurous spirit would have fit right in with this gang from Snug Harbor.

I admired Lillian Morrison in those days when I faced middle age and the empty nest. Older women of imagination and undying curiosity encouraged me to seek answers for myself in order to appreciate senior-citizenship. The real Lillian was the widow of a doctor in Colorado Springs. My Lillian comes as close to the real one as I can make her.

The central character of this story could have been Florence Means, Fran Bayless, Vesta Tutt, my own grandmother, any of my sisters, countless others. Blessed are the women who understand the importance of the rapture of being alive — at any age.

Frances Weaver

Pueblo, Colorado
May, 1992

CONTENTS

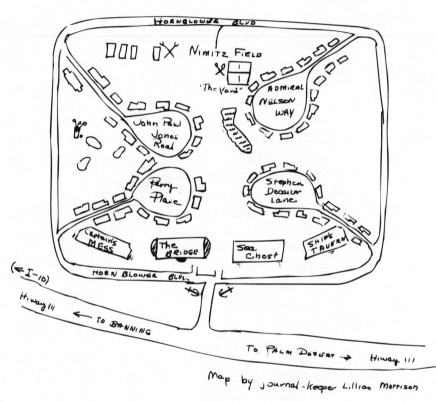

Map by Journal-Keeper Lillian Morrison

SNUG HARBOR, CALIFORNIA

GIRLS' DAY OUT

Bess Ferguson will be honking out in front in one hour. That will signify several things:

It's nine o'clock.

It's Bess's turn to drive to Redlands.

Ruth Coleman will be coming down her sidewalk.

Emmett Coleman will be glaring at Ruth.

George Schroeder will be walking toward the bus stop.

Today is Tuesday.

Well, I have myself all set and ready to go.

Bess and Ruth and I began making these weekly treks to Redlands almost a year ago. I can look up the exact date in my journal, of course. We like Redlands because of its settled old neighborhoods and its feeling of better days in Southern California. By "better" I mean less crowded, I guess. There are still a few groves around. The old houses on Fern and Olive Streets make me feel that I'm on my way to visit somebody's aunt.

Actually, Bess did have some relatives in Redlands at one time — her mother's family, I believe. We enjoy the time away from Snug Harbor once a week, anyway, and the hairdressers charge a lot less than the celebrity-type shops in Palm Springs do. So that's why we go, I suppose.

Not too warm today. That will make it even nicer. Just warm enough to eat outside at a fine little deli we've found where we can watch the traffic. Thank God there's not much traffic in Redlands. San Bernardino seems to have the corner on the market for traffic and smog. We drove over there just once and turned right around.

Before I sign off this entry to the endless journal, I'd better finish off yesterday, Monday.

❧

Not much of interest in the mail. I've finally stopped subscribing to the Colorado Springs paper. The news looks the same in any paper. I've read only the obituary column for the past year, so I just said, "Whoa, Lillian! You don't need this, even if you don't get anything else in the mail some days." So I quit. The kids call me when an old friend dies and my sisters keep me up on the gossip.

The book luncheon wasn't half bad. Maybe one of these days I'll go on a dig. That young man with his new book about old pots whetted my appetite for finding some of those things myself. In the back of this journal I keep a "maybe someday . . ." list. I'll put "dig" there. Perhaps some grandchild would like to go.

I didn't get that much of a kick from the craft session, I must admit. Mrs. Brinkley seems worn out on her shells-and-thongs routine. Any day now she'll go back to the macaroni-jewelry bit. Yesterday she tried to show us how to thread the leather thongs through glass beads to make a pattern. Howard Lanning told her she'd be better off with a kindergarten class learning colors. Lucille sent Howard off to shuffleboard. She left soon afterward herself.

Once in a while I wonder about the Lannings. He's such a loud-mouth and she can act really weird — peculiar, at least. Like showing up for bingo wearing her old fur jacket in case the air conditioning bothers her.

Anyway, that takes care of Monday for this week.

There's Bess. I'll finish this later. Journal-writing serves more as a time-filler than anything else around here, so this can wait.

❧

Do you recall my saying (writing) that I only write in this journal in the morning, when it's too early to do anything else? Well, strike that. Right now the clock on my mantelpiece from the old Hardy's Jewelry Store is bonging out eight o'clock, and that's P.M.

Right. I am journalizing at night because I'm afraid I'll forget some of today while I sleep. I don't want to forget today.

Bess honked right on cue at nine. Emmett put on his usual show when Ruth came out of their casita.

"How long will you women be gone?"

Then, more of the same old song and dance.

"Why can't you get your hair done right here? Nothing so special about those beauty operators, is there?"

And Emmett's famous last words:

"Just what do you expect me to do while you're out gallivanting all the hell and gone over Southern California?"

Ruth's smile never changed. She always has the answers ready since she always knows the questions. Has known for a year, now. Maybe Ruth has had the same answers for fifty years, who knows?

Anyway, Ruth looked particularly nice this morning in a becoming dress and sweater outfit she'd ordered from Brownstone — soft spring colors. She turned around to face her husband, just as she does every week, and shot answers back at him:

"We plan to be back before three."

"Hairdressers charge an absolute fortune around Palm Springs."

Then:

"I showed you where your lunch is all ready in the refrigerator. Just stick it in the toaster oven for five minutes and you'll be all set. There are biscuits left from breakfast on the counter."

Ruth always held the car door open one last minute for her parting shot.

"There seems to be a nice group of men who lunch together at the Mess on Tuesdays. Why don't you go over there?"

"One of these days, Ruth, you're going to choke on that line about the nice group of men lunching at the Mess," Bess said as she pulled away from the curb. I was sitting in the back seat. I couldn't help chuckling.

Now, I'm going to put an editorial note in here for anyone who might read this journal. I do that quite a bit, but my audience seems to consist entirely of my daughter and me, so far.

Today's note: *Because of unusual occurrences during this day, I will be writing dialogue into this journal.*

The journal-purists of the world might strangle in great fits over this transgression, but that's their own problem. I cannot record what happened in Redlands and on the way back in some sort of esoteric terms about inner self and hidden agendas.

So here we go. Bess, Ruth and I are headed for Redlands, and you are welcome to come along for the ride.

❧

First of all, we saw George Schroeder walking along Hornblower Boulevard on his way to the bus stop. He always looks happier on Tuesdays and Fridays because those are his holidays — busman's holidays. George rides the bus twice a week. Sometimes in one direction. Sometimes in another. But George loves those "coaches." We've spotted him sometimes, always sitting right behind the driver, talking a blue streak. Probably about his stops in Pennsylvania: Annville, Lebanon, Hershey. We know that routine by heart.

Like she always does, Bess pulled up beside George and stuck her head out the window.

"Can we give you a lift, George? We're headed for Redlands this morning."

Just like always, George grinned and shook his head.

"Nó. Thank you kindly, Miss Ferguson. I'll leave the driving to Trailways today. Going over to Riverside. Nice park there, and the old Mission Inn."

George could be the archetypical Pennsylvania Dutchman—round face, sober demeanor. I half expect him to say something like, "it wonders me if it will make down rain," or to order shoo-fly pie at the Captain's Mess. If they had shoo-fly pie it wouldn't be as fine as Esther's. We can be sure of that. George gave us his bus (coach) operator wave and we were off.

The drive to Redlands takes just under an hour. Close to fifty miles, which makes it perfect for us. Plenty of time to catch up on our visiting but not long enough to get bored with the ride. Sitting right here at my desk at this unaccustomed hour, scribbling on this journal as fast as I can go, I know I'll never be bored on that road again. Not after today.

༄

Just get to the point, Lil!" My husband used to yell that at me all the time. But I think details make a better story. However, we can skip over the hairdresser part except that in the parking lot we all got the giggles watching a darling little nun riding a three-wheeled bike with a big basket on it. Ruth said she'd seen her before, but Bess and I stared. Not any bigger than a minute, but she could get that clumsy bike up and down the hills around there like a teen-ager. I never can guess the ages of nuns, particularly the few left who wear the full habit. But this tiny person had to be in her seventies, at least.

We did a little shopping, no buying. Then we went to our favorite deli and sat out for a really great lunch. Bess sat there gazing into space.

"You know, not far from here I bet I could show you girls an old mansion where my cousins and sisters and I used to play," Bess said. "Nobody lived there. We could roam around and peek in the windows and pretend we were movie stars who owned such a grand place. On Sunset Drive, maybe. I'd almost forgotten about that. Instead of driving out around the university and all that, how about exploring?"

That suited me fine, of course. I didn't have a husband to worry about any longer, but Ruth had a kind of skeptical look.

"If it doesn't make us late," she said. "You know how Emmett gets if we're not back by three."

Did we ever know how "Emmett gets"! Just once last May was enough for Bess and me.

Bess paid for lunch from our Girls' Day Out kitty. We had decided from the very first of these outings that we'd have a Tuesday fund, which we all shared. Kind of funny how it started. After our first lunch together, each of us reached for our purse. Then we heard a bunch of old ladies at the next table splitting their bill. One old gal had a high, squawky voice. She bellered something about "Georgene had the crab salad." Didn't take the three of us long to work out our finances better than that!

Driving through the old, rich-folks' part of Redlands was a joy. Bess kept saying, "Now, I remember . . ."

Just as we headed up Sunset, however, we all yelled at once. There beside the road knelt our little nun. The chain had slipped off her bike and she was struggling to get it back in place.

Bess stopped immediately, of course, and we all jumped out. In less time than it takes to tell it, my two friends were down on the ground beside Sister Anne. (She told us her name later, but we felt then as if we knew her.)

You never saw such a smile! She absolutely beamed when she realized we wanted to help. I just stood there. What do I know about chains on bicycles? I did think I might direct traffic if another car came along. Bess and Ruth were having the times of their lives.

Ruth introduced the three of us. "We noticed you and your bike at the shopping center earlier, Sister. You ride extremely well." You could tell she stopped just short of saying, ". . . for a woman your age." Sister Anne could tell that, too. She nodded at all of us.

"I ride down every morning to the post office to collect the mail for the convent and to run a few errands as I need to. This chain slips every

once in a while. It's not far up to the convent from here and I often have
to walk the bike back up to where Mike can fix it for me. How nice for
me this afternoon that you ladies came along! The walk all the way up
can be wearing in the heat of the day."

Bess soon had the chain on where it belonged. She wiped her
hands on her blue denim skirt and gave the tiny nun a big grin.

"Sister, I'd like to test-drive this chain to make sure it's okay now.
We don't want you having any spills. I haven't ridden a bike like this in
years, but what do you say you ride on up the hill with my two friends
in the car and I'll follow on your velocipede, here? Okay? Ruth, the keys
are in the ignition."

That Holy Sister fairly radiated when Bess suggested that.

The drive on up Sunset wound past eucalyptus trees and tangled
old oleanders. Some spacious, fancy houses lined the avenue until we
got near the top, where a long stucco wall in need of many repairs cut
off the view of the grounds inside. Right ahead of us I could see a huge
pink mansion-type structure. I leaned up to tap Ruth on the shoulder.

"Do you suppose that's the mansion Bess used to play around?
Looks pretty deserted to me."

Sister Anne was so short I couldn't even see her from the back seat.
"Straight ahead?" Now I could see her bony finger, pointing.

"That, ladies, is our convent. Our order is St. Ives. Of course, this is
not the Mother House. That's in upstate New York. Mr Burrage built
this house here in Redlands many years ago — a real showplace, I'd say.
He left the property to the church. Bless him, but the upkeep has been
almost too much for the sisterhood these past years."

You can say that again, I thought. The whole place had turned into
a jungle. We drove up the drive past the biggest barn this side of Santa
Anita, and I figured it would take a machete and six bulldozers to clear
a path to where the tennis courts must have been. No wonder old
Burrage left it to the church. His kids surely didn't want it, and in the
depression nobody would buy a white elephant like this.

That was mean of me to think that way. Still, I could see what must
have been so wonderful to Bess when she was a kid.

Bess was all tuckered out, as they might say back in Kansas City,
when she reached the top of that hill. "Little lady, you are some cyclist!"
she gasped at Sister Anne.

Ruth picked up the sacks in the basket behind the seat. "Nothing in
here but cat food," she whispered to me. "Do you have the mail in this
sack, Sister?" she said, aloud.

Sister Anne forced her magic smile. "There wasn't any."

At the sound of Sister's voice, cats appeared as if on cue. Cats came from everywhere! The barn, the weeds, the porches, the terrace over-looking Redlands and the valley — all alive with cats. Any color, any size, any stage of pregnancy.

Sister Anne bent to touch each one as the cats surrounded her in the drive. "Order of St. Ives," she said with a smile.

Well, Ruth kept checking her watch, so Bess and I knew we had to cut this short. We refused the offer of a conducted tour of the decrepit mansion but promised to return the next Tuesday, earlier in the day. "Why don't you wait for us next Tuesday, Sister? That way you can ride with us and give your bike a rest." Bess really has a way with words, doesn't she?

Hell-bent for Snug Harbor, we hoped to be no more than fifteen minutes late at the most. Emmett would be standing out by their mailbox. Damn.

Note: I am sixty-nine. Have I told you that? In my first sixty-nine years I have learned just two really good lessons.

The first: Don't sweat the small stuff.

The second: Don't expect the rest of the world to do what you know you have to do for yourself.

Simple? It works for me so far, even if it took me most of three score and ten to figure that much out. So here I am, sixty-nine years old, still up 'way past my usual bedtime, scribbling away here so I won't forget the details of this extraordinary day.

You might have thought that the meeting-the-nun story was what made Tuesday a big day, but that was only the first half. Believe me, it gets even better!

❧

About halfway home to Snug Harbor, between Beaumont and Banning, we were zipping along I-10. Bess was really pushing, trying to get Ruth home before Emmett exploded. All of a sudden she slammed on the brakes and almost swerved off the road. Ruth and I had been chatting, trying not to put any more pressure on Bess. Generally speaking, Bess is a careful driver. We all are. Not that we are protecting our lives so much; we just want these cars to last. So this maneuver of Bess's brought us to attention in a hurry. I almost said, "What the hell!" but Ruth beat me to it. I realized I was shaking.

"Over there! Look back! No, on the other side of the road — the other lane! See him? George! George Schroeder! Our friend George!" Bess was certainly worked up. I had never seen her so excited before.

She had slowed now to make an illegal U-turn to get into the westbound lane back toward Beaumont.

"See him, Ruth?" She had scared the daylights out of two Toyotas and a Chevy pickup by careening across three lanes of traffic in front of them to get to the far right lane.

"You mean that man standing beside that big bus?"

"Are you sure that's Schroeder?" I asked, because Ruth and I were not sure of anything. Bess might have flipped out at the prospect of facing Emmett being mad at us again.

I tried to be the calm one. "Now, what would a meek and mild little man like George Schroeder be doing standing out on a superhighway in all of this traffic, waving his arms like a madman and pointing to a hellishly big bus? Bess, are you sure — ?"

Bess didn't have to answer. By that time she had pulled up behind the bus and jumped out of her car. Thank heaven she ran to the right side of the bus away from the roaring, speeding traffic! (I remember thinking, is that starboard?) Sure enough, here came George, looking as if he had spent all day in a demolition derby. He was beat.

"Oh, I just prayed you ladies would come along! Thank you! Thank you for stopping! I need your help! I *do* need your help!"

Ruth looked like she might faint. One more delay and Emmett —

"Now, George, just calm down here a bit and get your breath." Bess patted his arm. "The girls and I are on our way home, but we'll do what we can. First, in one short sentence, what's the problem?"

George took a deep breath, which almost did him in. "That coach!" He pointed, as if we might not have noticed that he was jumping like a puppet next to one gigantic "cruiser."

"That coach broke down this morning! The driver was a young twerp who had no appreciation for such a fine piece of — "

"Easy, here, George! Just the pertinent facts. So the bus won't go. Now what on earth does that have to do with us? I figured you need a ride home. That's why I stopped. Is there more to the story?" Bess Ferguson must have been a fine teacher. No wonder her girls won the tournaments.

"Sure, there's more to the story!" I guess you could say George just blurted that out. "The dumb-bunny rookie operator left me to guard this coach while he went off to call the dispatcher for help. That was almost six hours ago! The other passengers — I'll tell you about them later — now it's been six hours and not one soul has showed up! I don't think he even called! Probably scared they'd fire him, so he quit and walked away! That's my guess! These youngsters have no idea of the value of — "

"George!" I had to interrupt. We had to get home.

"Okay. I must protect this coach until it can be returned to the company barns. It's only a vapor lock. This baby will run fine, now. All I need to do is move her out of harm's way. If we let her stay here all night she'll be vandalized by morning — tires slashed, windows shattered. These Californians are crazy!"

Well, he's just a short little Pennsylvania Dutchman, and a lonely one at that, but as George got that gleam in his eye I knew no bus ever had a more dedicated protector than this one right here.

Ruth had long since stopped worrying about what Emmett might say. She already knew, anyway. "George," she said carefully, "You have spent the entire day contemplating this bus and this predicament. What do you suggest? What is the next move?"

"Ah, Ruth! Good question!" Never before had he called her by her first name. Or by any name, for that matter. "See that shed, that packing barn, over there? Just off the access? Looks to me as if that place is empty and will just about fit this vehicle. If we could arrange to leave her there for the night I could drive her over myself. Then tomorrow morning we could decide how best to — "

"Great." Bess had had enough conversation. "I'll go talk to the man I see out in front there and then signal you to drive on over. I suppose you've driven lots of busses this size, haven't you, George?"

"Oh, no, Miss Ferguson. All my life I've dreamed of driving the Interstate. Now, thinking of driving this beauty just around the corner to that — Esther would be so proud!"

"Just don't cry, George," I whispered to Ruth. "I don't think I can take watching a grown man cry over a vapor-locked bus."

～

We were back in the car and Bess was rehearsing her speech to the owner of the barn. At the same time I had a feeling Bess was tumbling a lot of other thoughts about busses around in her brain. Made me think of the rock tumbler John bought for the kids and set it up in our garage. For months on end that contraption sat there, tumbling rocks, and nobody ever opened it to see what had happened to the rocks. Just gazing at the back of Bess's head, I could tell her tumbler was about to come up with some sort of a polished gem of an idea. Somehow, that gave me the shivers.

Bess and Ruth worked the deal about the barn. I stayed in the car, thinking about whatever could be done with a forty-six-passenger bus that might fall into one's possession like manna from heaven.

My two companions were so animated in their negotiations with the brusque, dirty barnkeeper that I could almost guess what they were thinking, too.

Abruptly, Bess pulled out our Girls' Day Out purse and gave the man all the money we had left. *Hey*, I almost yelled, *that's our lunch money for the next six weeks!* But Ruth and Bess were both waving wildly at George over on the highway, so I kept quiet.

We all watched almost reverently as George Schroeder wheeled that enormous baby into that narrow garage with inches to spare on either side. "You're so right, George. Esther would be most proud," I said to nobody in particular.

❧

N ow it's really late. I'll have to tell you in the morning about the conversation on the ride home and Emmett's tantrum later. This probably won't make sense when I read it over tomorrow, but at least I've got most of the day on paper.

Quite a day for a bunch of old fogies washed ashore at Snug Harbor!

❧

SHIPSHAPE LEISURE LIVING

Y ou need to know more about Snug Harbor. If I'm going to devote the next few weeks to telling you about the goings-on around this place, you ought to have a good picture of it in your head. Every time I say, "We walked down past the Sea Chest," you need to know that that only means that we passed the gift shop without having to look at the map in the front of the book — if this bunch of drivel ever becomes a book.

You probably wonder why a place this close to Palm Springs should be named Snug Harbor. Good question! The Skipper named this place when he decided to build a retirement village here. Actually, the Skipper won this land in a crap game in Manila about thirty years ago and never really laid eyes on it 'til he retired about ten years ago. He had some wild idea he could build a bunch of little houses here, decorate the patios with big ropes, call everything some Navy name, and attract all the retired Navy personnel on the West Coast. What he didn't take into consideration was that most of those men had stayed in the Navy because they loved water. Not sand.

The Skipper is not what you'd call a quick study. Give him a Navy manual of some sort, he knows it all. But give him anything new to think about, he hides behind the authority he had in his uniform and *pretends* to know it all. You know the kind. So the Skipper commands this retirement village as if he were still shouting orders on the deck of a destroyer. Chief Petty Officer, that's his rank. And petty is the right word.

You'll see him around once in a while. He's the one with the pot belly and the beat-up white cap with the gold on the front. It says "Sea World," if you look close. Generally he's yelling about something, but I'll give the man credit: When he realized this was no magnet for old sailors, he went out and found plenty of us landlubbers to fill the gaps.

The Skipper runs a tight ship. The grounds are always policed up and the brightwork on the doors to the Bridge and the Captain's Mess shines better than some of the five-star hotels my husband and I loved to stay in years ago. Brightwork is navy talk for the polished brass door handles, hinges, and all that.

Place names do surprise some of our visitors. The Bridge, you see, houses the offices. That's where they keep the machinery that runs this ship, as some comedian loved to say. You face that building as you drive through the gates with the big anchors and the chains.

We're on route 111 just off I-10 about two miles. Good location. The Bridge has that stucco-Spanish look because that's the way the builder insisted on making it, but the Skipper has garnished it with figureheads on the corners of the deck all around, and the portholes instead of windows on most of the public buildings match the ones on our cottages. You might have noticed that.

Just starboard of the Bridge, that's the Sea Chest. It might seem funny to have so many potted palms around the Sea Chest, but the Skipper says they remind him of the palm tree in *Mister Roberts*. Personally, I hadn't made the connection until he pointed it out on my get-acquainted rounds. There's a small galley at the far end of the Sea Chest where snacks and cold drinks are available whenever. Then, following the red and green running lights — they mark port and starboard, naturally — you'll see the Ship's Tavern. Game room, auditorium and all that.

You probably noticed that Hornblower Boulevard makes a complete circle. That's our main thoroughfare. You can't get lost, especially with the green lights always to starboard (I think). At least it's a one-way street! We all live on small culs-de-sac with nautical names. Most of my friends and I live on Stephen Decatur Lane. He was the hero on the shores of Tripoli, according to the Skipper, but not according to the Marines. Oh, well.

Next street off Hornblower is Admiral Nelson Way. Then you pass the pool and the rec center. We just call that area the Yard. Not many serious swimmers here, and that's a good thing. The Skipper allowed himself a flight of whimsy in designing the pool. It's the same shape as California. Once in a while Bess Ferguson forgets about that and beans herself on the Monterey Peninsula. Nobody dares to laugh when that happens, but once Howard Lanning almost drowned of apoplexy trying to stop giggling over at the deep end. That's Baja.

Now, if you walk on around here — the whole circle is about three-quarters of a mile — you'll come to John Paul Jones Road. You go through that entrance to the three-putt golf course. Shuffleboard is on down a ways closer to Nimitz. That one more street is Perry, just by the Captain's Mess, which serves really fine food. We all have our own galleys in our quarters, of course, but once in a while we eat together at the Mess. Good Sunday brunch, of course, when most of us have visitors, if we have any visitors at all.

❧

You're looking at me like you're confused about all the port and starboard and all that. Undoubtedly you're dying to ask me one question but hesitate because it might sound rude. Especially asking an old woman like me. Go ahead. I won't mind. You want to know why a dignified old dame like me would choose to live in a settlement in the heart of the desert with Navy symbolism and a Skipper wearing a Sea World cap.

Well, the answer is simple. You see, after forty-five years of being married to a dignified surgeon, living in a proper neighborhood, serving on every known committee west of any given point, giving book reviews and narrating fashion shows all over Colorado and most of New Mexico, after spending "vacation" time listening to doctors telling other doctors how brilliant they were over and over again, after my kids were on their own and my place of residence became my own concern, I saw this place and fell for it.

I am through with stodgy. I'm a widow living on my own now. I'm my own boss now. I have had it with proper. Snug Harbor looked like fun to me when I first saw it and, believe me, Snug Harbor will be fun before I'm through. Even if it's fun only in my journals.

❧

NOBODY RAISES CAIN LIKE AN IOWA FARMER!

May I share a little something with you, please? Before I went to bed last night, after writing in this journal 'til almost midnight about the nun and the bus and all that from yesterday, which I have yet to finish, I was reminded of some dopey poems I'd put in my journal about four months ago. My stuff isn't generally of rereadable quality. I just write down how I feel about the world in general. But the thought of those poor poems nagged at me before I went to sleep. How about this:

> *Living in retirement*
> *Without enough to do*
> *Is giving me the feeling*
> *Of inhabiting a zoo.*

I suppose I used "zoo" because of being safe inside while the world goes on by. I even wrote more:

> *I'm cared for,*
> *fed and watered;*
> *I have my own safe bed.*
> *My days are endlessly the same —*
> *The sameness that I dread.*

Now, when I was entertaining such dismal thoughts a few months ago, is it any wonder that I'm intrigued with what might happen around here?

About the bus, I mean. But I have not told you all that.

Bess and Ruth arranged with the man with the empty barn to let

George put the bus in there to protect it from vandals. The guy was not dumb. He charged fifty dollars for the first night and said he'd need that much every day. But the bus had to be out of there inside of two weeks. In two weeks the barn will be torn down, and that won't take more than ten minutes, if you ask me.

Anyway, without any kind of guarantee that the fellow won't just drive off in that bus and we'll never see it again, we drove merrily on our way back to Snug Harbor. And we were all as high as kites. Excited as kids who know a secret.

I did try to calm George down a bit in the back seat.

"George," I said, "How do you know that man back there isn't already reporting to the police about that vehicle and claiming you stole it? He might turn us in. Better still, he might turn the bus in and claim a reward from Trailways. Think about that."

"Because you ladies paid him cash and he has no idea who we are or where we live."

"He undoubtedly has my license number, George," Bess said.

But there was no stopping George. Now that I look at those pathetic attempts at poetry, I see why I was so excited about the whole proposition. Of course, we all kind of kept our thoughts to ourselves about how we could use that vehicle until just before Bess turned into the front gate. Maybe it was the sight of those huge anchors and all that big chain that did it. All four of us started talking at once.

Ruth said, "We all talk about travel and such, wouldn't it be grand if we could all travel to favorite places together?"

Bess said, "That great coach would take us anyplace in the USA we want to go. To get away from here for a while . . ."

George said, "By the time we'd get to Pennsylvania the dogwood could be blooming."

I chimed in something about the joy of travel in expanding one's horizons, or some such. I don't know why I always think I have to sound so brainy. All I really thought about was the fun it would be to take a marvelous excursion on a stolen bus. A bus George just happened to be left in charge of. Thank God the last passenger aboard hadn't been Emmett!

Emmett. That brought us up short. We all checked our watches as if on command. Five o'clock. Never before had we been this late. There he stood by the mailbox. Arms crossed. Hat pulled down over his eyes.

Ruth sighed. "We cannot talk about this with Emmett tonight." We nodded as if our heads were all attached to one string. "Why don't the three of you come over about ten tomorrow morning? I'll bake some of his favorite cookies. Then we can talk. And at bingo tomorrow night . . ."

Bess patted Ruth's arm. "One high hurdle at a time, Ruthie. See you tomorrow at ten."

That's when I came home and started to write as soon as I finished my supper. Excited? I could hardly eat or sleep.

And now it's about ten — ten o'clock on the most exhilarating morning I've had since Joanie and her kids were here in April. This morning, waking up early was not just a pleasure, it was a necessity. I had to gather my thoughts for this confrontation with Emmett Coleman.

George will come past my house on the way to the Colemans. I think we'd best get there together. I'm going to take notes. Don't want to leave out anything when I report back to you. This will be a memorable morning.

Before I leave my desk, I'd like to share a couple more lines of my limp poetry from that other journal:

> *The others in the Harbor*
> *Are neighbors, not close friends.*

We'll soon see about that.

❧

"Well, Mrs. Morrison, did you sleep well?" George seemed to be his polite, timid self as we started to cross Decatur.

"Of course not, George. Just the excitement of yesterday has my adrenalin going — might even have raised my blood pressure a bit. I slept in fits and starts, mostly composing more arguments for Emmett whenever I wakened. He can be a very stubborn man. I gather he's had his own way most of his life — like most of the men our age, particularly anyone independent enough to be a farmer. And I'm not even certain what we want to say to him. After all, we have only the germ of an idea here."

One whiff of Ruth's cookies fresh from the oven told us she was happy to see us, anyway. Bess had arrived just as George and I left my house. On such a bright morning, the Colemans' living room had the warmth of a farmhouse in Iowa. Family pieces of furniture, a small oak table and chairs in the dining ell, chintz sofa and comfortable arm chairs all well lived-in and loved. One of the joys of Snug Harbor seems to me to be the way you can see each person's life in whatever they choose to move here. This room reflected Ruth's good taste and homemaking skills.

My euphoria didn't last long. Ruth brought the cookies to the coffee table, where the pot and cups were laid out for us. Before she could even say, "would you like a cookie?" Emmett had taken a stance in front of the fireplace.

Emmett is not long on formalities. In his usual outfit, freshly ironed khaki pants and shirt, uniform of the Iowa farmer, he could have been addressing a Grange meeting about the damaging effect of erosion on corn fields. I noticed how red his forehead was. Usually it's whiter than the rest of his face, since he never goes anywhere without that goofy straw hat.

"If you people think for one minute I will take part in any sort of subterfuge involving a contraband Trailways bus, you are badly mistaken. If you for one instant think I will allow my wife to take part in any such nonsense, you are doubly out of your minds. If you have any idea of getting aboard that purloined vehicle and gallivanting all over the country, running the risk of being arrested, convicted and sentenced to a federal penitentiary since you intend to cross state lines, you will do that without the assistance, help or previous knowledge of the Emmett Colemans. If you came here for the purpose of promoting such a scheme, you are in the wrong place and you might just as well go on about your crazy scheming elsewhere!"

Damn, I thought. This man is 'way ahead of us. Ruth couldn't have told him we were planning a trip on this bus. We didn't even say that — not in so many words — to each other! But here he goes ranting and raving about what we haven't even asked him yet!

None of us had ever heard Emmett string together so many words at once. I had not been sure he even knew some of those words. By the time he finished this spiel, his whole face was bright red and his eyes seemed to bug out a bit. Ruth, standing near the kitchen door, could have been close to tears.

The rest of us — Bess, George and I — sat staring first at him and then at our shoes. We probably looked for all the world like a bunch of kids begging to keep the puppy that had followed us home. Only we didn't have a puppy to beg for. We had a forty-six-passenger bus.

All Ruth could say was, "Now, Emmett." Not much help.

Bess recovered her bearing first. "Emmett, we appreciate your

thoughts. Obviously Ruth has told you the basic story here. Inciden-
tally, please accept our apologies for being so late yesterday. We shall
not let that happen again. And Ruth has undoubtedly told you about
Sister Anne." From his glare, I could tell that Emmett cared even less for
nuns than he did for gym teachers.

Not much stops Bess when she has something to say. "Each one of
us here at Snug Harbor has expressed in one way or another our sense
of futility, of being disappointed with the monotony of our lives here.
We often have spoken of favorite places and remembered sights of our
travels and our home country. Many of us would delight in a brief
return to old haunts, so to speak. And now we have this bus —"

"Now *we* have this bus?" roared Emmett. The MGM lion never
made such a noise. "*We?* Who are you calling *we*, Miss Ferguson? The
bus belongs to Trailways. Paying some stranger fifty bucks to hide it for
you does not make that broken-down bus yours, and certainly not
mine. And more especially, not my wife's."

George couldn't stand the way Emmett was yelling at the rest of us.
He had started twitching, almost dropping his cookie.

"You should see that beauty, Coleman. Looks brand new. Only
problem I can find is vapor lock. You and I know enough about motors
to fix that. Besides, we wouldn't be going where it's all that warm.
California sunshine and desert heat can get old. We could take this
baby to Yellowstone, or even the East Coast."

"You can do most anything if you eat regular, Schroeder." Actually,
Emmett used a more crude farm-type expression, but I prefer not to
put that into my journal in case some child might pick it up. "Just count
me out. And Ruth."

I realized all eyes were on me, Emmett frowning, the others expectant. How could they expect me to convince this man of anything? After
all, I had lived with a surgeon for forty-six years. I know how things go
when a man makes up his mind: backwards.

"Try to look at this situation from our point of view for just a
minute, Emmett. Nobody says much about it, but the biggest problem
in an idyllic setting like this place is boredom. Boredom is ninety-nine
percent self-inflicted. Don't ever forget that, Emmett. Now, you break
up the monotony of your days with hoeing in your small garden. Good
for you. Often I am tempted to come along just to watch you hoe."

Emmett snorted. I hoped it was a good sign.

"This is not peculiar to Snug Harbor. Every place like this provides
activities, but sooner or later the sameness sets in. What we have here

is an opportunity for an adventure unparalleled in retirement-village annals, as far as I'm concerned. In spite of the hazards involved — *because* of the hazards —we might wind up having one fine time out of this. It seems almost providential that the bus without a driver and the convent with a barn should burst upon our horizon at the same time." Damn. I hadn't meant to be so flowery.

Well, at least Emmett had shut up for a while. Now he pursed his lips, gave Ruth a withering glance, and strode out of the room. We heard the back door slam and the rattle of rake and hoe in the carport. Emmett's garden would be twice-hoed today.

"I hope you all know Emmett well enough to understand . . ." Ruth looked sick.

Bess helped herself to one more of those fine date cookies and I followed suit. Much as I try to stay away from sweets and take off a pound or twenty, in times of stress nothing soothes more than a home-baked cookie, unless it's a Milky Way. That cookie hit the spot.

George certainly was not the clear-eyed, pink-cheeked Dutchman who had walked over there with me. He seemed to have aged twenty years in ten minutes. The old slump of the shoulders had returned; his sweater drooped more than ever. Finally, he finished his coffee, set the cup on the table, and stood up. Still the shortest person in the room.

"Ruth," he almost whispered, "I do hope we haven't caused too much trouble here. With your husband, I mean. He has a right to his opinions, I know. But I had hoped we could talk to the rest of our table tonight at bingo, and if Emmett starts right out — well, I understand if he doesn't want to be involved, but do you suppose he'll . . . ?"

"George, I make no promises about Emmett's behavior, ever. But I am relatively sure he will not go storming into bingo ranting and raving about what we hope to be able to do with our bus. You notice I said, 'we hope.' Don't count me out. Emmett was wagonmaster at our house mostly because we never had any children to share the burdens or the joys, and because his mother lived with us in her old age for nearly thirty years. Maybe it's time for Emmett to find out his wife has a mind of her own." Ruth paused. "Or maybe it's about thirty years too late."

❧

ow busy are you today, George?" I asked the question as we walked back to my place. Bess walked along. "Busy? Me? You're making a joke, Mrs. Morrison. Time I have more of than anything. I might go to photography this afternoon, but that doesn't start 'til three. Busy? Me?"

"Fine. Bess, what can we do to further this cause, strengthen our hand, before we talk to anyone else?"

Bess thought about it. "I'd say we ought to move the bus before we owe the man next year's lunch money, too. And the best way to do that is to catch Sister Anne. Even if we don't get this project off the ground, having the bus in her barn will give us breathing space. After this session, I'm sure we'll need a lot of that."

" Then, *don't pass go. Don't collect two hundred dollars.* Let's get right into my car and head back to Redlands. You drove yesterday, Bess, and you'll have to— You'll have to operate the coach, George. My car this time."

For some reason, the rest of that silly quote about the two hundred dollars from the Monopoly game flipped up in my head like the titles on an old movie screen:

Go directly to jail.

And off we went to Redlands.

⟿

"O-67"   "Oh"

"B-6"   "Oh, Oh"

'N-35'   "Oh my!"

"G-51"   "Wow!"

"I-22"   "BINGO!!"

BINGO!

Whatever happened to the old lady who was sitting at this desk three days ago bemoaning the fact that she had too little to occupy her time and her mind?

Whatever happened to the old gal who agreed with Helen Trent that ". . . life had passed her by after thirty-five?"

Who is this considering investing in a word-processor — a laptop, yet — in order to keep up with her journal entries?

Who just barely got back from Redlands in time for photography class, then raced home to record the day's happenings before dashing off to bingo? After all, it's Wednesday, already! Where has the time gone?

Whatever happened came in two parts. You know that — the nun and the bus. Or vice versa. At any rate, here's what went on after we (George and Bess and I) recovered from the tongue-lashing administered by the immovable Mr. Coleman. I told the others while we were on our way to Redlands that Emmett reminds me of my husband's favorite slogan about himself: "often in error but never in doubt." At least, John had sense enough to acknowledge such a trait in himself. Not Emmett.

❧

As you will realize more and more as I tell you about Bess Ferguson, she has an uncanny ability to figure "the Best Way" for accomplishing almost anything. She should have been a politician, or at least a specialist in labor relations.

Headed for Redlands to try to strike some sort of a nun-stores-stolen-bus deal, Bess rode in the back seat, not saying a word. Just as we passed the barn between Beaumont and Banning, Bess leaned forward to make sure George and I could hear her. We had been pretty quiet, too.

"Let's stop at our deli and pick up some sandwiches before we go to the convent. That way we can pretend we need to have a picnic there and we'll just happen to have a sandwich for Sister and a few thousand scraps for the cats. I would hate to embarrass that dear soul by appearing just at lunch time when it looks like she has barely enough to feed herself. Do nuns get Social Security?" Bless Bess.

We found Sister Ann just ready to set out on her bike. You should have seen the look on George's face when he first saw that blessed creature! He was totally charmed from the start. I had had the feeling George had grown up among the "plain people" and had not had much confidence in anyone involved in Holy Orders, but clearly George judges not lest he be judged. Or some such relevant statement. Even the onslaught of cats failed to ruffle George. At the sight of that barn, an onslaught of alligators would not have ruffled George.

Bess carried out the introductions, then turned on her old Kansas City gym-teacher charm. Her short-cropped gray hair caught the sunlight and her dark eyes shone with such enthusiasm! She might have been talking the school board into buying new basketball uniforms.

Hands on hips, she smiled. "Sister, Mrs. Morrison and I were just telling Mr. Schroeder about our chance meeting with you yesterday so we decided to drop by. Why don't you let us drive you on your errands today? We'd love to get better acquainted and to know more about your order and your mission here." She let that sink in.

"Besides, Sister, we have a favor to ask of you, so we'd like to reciprocate in advance by doing something for you. Is going for the mail your task every day, or do the other sisters take turns?"

Already Bess was opening the back door of my car for our passenger.

"Oh, yes, my dears, this became my daily task almost two years ago when Sister Cleone died. She and I were the only ones left here, and until the Mother House has someone else to assist in keeping our mission going, the responsibility is mine. Doing the Lord's work can be lonely at times, but as long as I have Mike to help out in emergencies and the cats to keep me company, and the lovely view from the top of our hill, I do manage. Besides, riding that three-wheeler keeps me in shape."

Bess nodded. "You're in better shape than I am. I found that out about half-way up your hill yesterday."

Sister Anne had settled into my back seat and seemed even smaller than in Bess's front seat, when I couldn't even see her head.

"Now. You mentioned favors. Of course I shall be happy to be of any help I can, but whatever on earth can I do for people like you?"

"We'll get into that later, Sister," Bess answered. "Shall we head for the post office first?"

No trouble there. Back down the curving road to the center of Redlands. The post office is a handsome California-Spanish building, a remnant of the days when California basked in Spanish heritage and post offices were built to be impressive, not simply functional. Collecting the mail did not take long. There wasn't any.

"I guess that really is all I need to do today," the good Sister said, seemingly unperturbed by the lack of any correspondence. "I bought cat food for my darlings yesterday, and I have a fine supply of candles the Altar Guild ladies from St. Pius brought. That's all I need."

Not even a box of Oreos? Our next Redlands excursion will include Ruth's date-filled cookies. This dear lady deserves the best.

"Now, what can I do for you?"

Bess answered. As you might have assumed from reading this journal, I had decided to let Bess do a lot of the talking as this possible plot developed. I've always been better at the follow-up. You soften 'em up, I'll go for the clincher. Besides, Bess is good.

"Actually, Sister, we have two favors to ask. We have brought along a picnic lunch and we hoped you might allow us to enjoy our sandwiches and the view of Redlands from this wonderful terrace — plus the pleasure of your company, of course. Mrs. Coleman couldn't be with us today, but she sent along some cookies for us to share with you along with these sandwiches."

Now how on earth did Bess manage that? She had her purse full of Ruth's cookies! I could smell them from the back seat. I tell you, that girl is good!

"Lunching with you three will surely be my pleasure, Miss Ferguson. But what else . . . ?"

"We need to rent your barn. That is, if you are not using all of the space in that glorious barn we would like to rent space for a week or two."

God bless you, Bess. Say just enough.

Well, the view does take your breath away, even if the terrace is knee-high in weeds and cats. We managed to enjoy a fine lunch sitting on a cracked concrete slab on which faded lines of a shuffleboard court could still be seen. Sister made no bones about relishing such food as we had from the deli.

"My vows don't allow me to indulge myself in such pleasures," she admitted, "but I have never had any qualms about accepting such treats from others. I feel I have other ways of repaying such gifts. Now, about renting the barn. Of course there's plenty of space there. It's a fine dry barn built for polo ponies and other such pets when Mr. Burrage had this place. Just what do you wish to store there?"

George coughed. As a matter of fact, George nearly choked on his liverwurst-on-pumpernickel.

Just don't get nervous and try the pickle right now, George, I thought.

"Sister Anne"—he cleared his throat—"Sister Anne, we have been granted the loan of a fine transcontinental coach — bus — by an anonymous benefactor. You know how that goes. And while we at Snug Harbor are deciding exactly how to make use of this fine windfall, we must store it out of harm's way. Not for long. Our plans are not finalized yet" — Bess and I glanced at each other, then stared at our shoes — "but we would appreciate your helping us with sanctuary for the coach to protect it from vandals and such. Your barn would be ideal —"

Time for me to butt in. "We did say 'rent,' Sister. Perhaps twenty or thirty dollars a day while we are in the process . . ."

"A *day*? *Every day*? Well, my dears, that barn is yours for as long as you need it." She sighed. "The Lord *does* work in strange ways! I can scarcely wait to report this good news back to the Mother House. When could you move the vehicle here? Mike can open the doors for us. He comes around every Wednesday, so we're in luck. Yes, I'd say we're all in luck. If I ever get back to the Mother House up in New York I shall tell the Mother Superior all about this fine day — even the elegant sand-wiches.

"You did say, Miss Ferguson, that you'd like to know more about our mission here. Could I persuade you to come along on my special guided tour? It won't take long. The upper floors are closed off since neither Mike nor I can negotiate the steps."

Just one step inside was enough for me. Bare cracked walls, hollow-sounding hallways, cavernous rooms with no furnishings, dust, and cats. We followed Sister Anne in absolute silence.

The breakfast room had been converted into a chapel. The adjoining butler's pantry had one small cot. The rest was empty. This nun needed help, no doubt about that!

Somehow, as I write this, I feel the pieces are falling into place too easily. Then I remember Emmett Coleman. Scratch the "too easily" part.

The rest went like clockwork, for this day, at least. We chased back to the barn. George had the keys in his hands the entire trip. He jingled them as we rode along. He kept humming, too. Finally, I asked what song that was and George burst out singing like a kid in the glee club:

> *For I want to hire out as the Skipper*
> *Who dodges life's stress and life's strains;*
> *Of the trolley, the Toonerville trolley,*
> *The trolley that meets all the trains.*

The tune sounded suspiciously like, *I used to work in Chicago*, but I kept quiet.

"That's a song my dad used to sing. He was a motorman. I guess you could say I'm about the third generation in my family in the transportation business. Esther and I always hoped Sonny would follow the family tradition, but he . . . married a California girl he met out here in the Navy. I tried to tell Esther — oh, well."

Sometimes old men are so much like little boys it can break your heart.

Our snarly "landlord" said almost nothing to us as we drove up to retrieve our bus. He must have been counting on renting to us for the entire two weeks until the barn would be demolished. George went right in as Bess and I stood to one side.

As soon as the coach (I must remember to use that term; George might read this some day) cleared the barn doors, George opened his window. "I'm going to open her doors, ladies. Climb aboard and have a look around. She's a real beauty."

From someplace he had found a driver's cap. The disgruntled young man must have left it. George had it square on his head — no rakish angle for our operator! With that cap on, our little Pennsylvania Dutch friend seemed to have grown at least four inches. His shoulders squared, his eyes literally sparkling, he looked like the album pictures he had shown us of himself, with Esther and Sonny, of course, standing beside a Lebanon Valley Transit vehicle.

("That snapshot was taken in Annville," George had told us, "Right by the Jerusalem Cemetery monument. That's where we had my retirement picnic. Handiest place for all my old passengers to come. Just two weeks before Esther got so sick . . .")

George ushered Bess and me onto that empty bus as though he were maitre d' at the Ritz seating some Mrs. Vanderbilt. We walked down the aisle, running our hands over the upholstery, checking the overhead racks. Bess even peeked into the rest room. George went forward and sat in the driver's seat, caressing the steering wheel and making cooing noises to the dashboard. He pushed on the pedals even though I doubted he could reach them. For the first time since Esther died, I'd judge, George has something to love and to care for. Bless him.

Finally, he pulled some mighty handle and air brakes whooshed. "Let's go, ladies. I'll follow you to the barn. I've turned the sign on the front to 'CHARTER' and I've got this cap. We'll get that far without a problem."

You know what? He was right. Nobody even noticed that bus behind us. "Bess, that is one fine motor vehicle back there," I told her. Bess just nodded and smiled.

Sister was slightly overwhelmed by such a monster. "Oh my!" she gasped. "You could take a lot of people almost anyplace on a splendid . . . coach . . . like that!" At that moment, George, Bess, and I knew we had signed on our first passenger.

❧

Nine-thirty p.m. Wednesday. Back from bingo, but I'm not sure how we did. Not the game: Mrs. Haley won three dollars. Par for the course. "Not sure" means I cannot decide if we potential mutineers made any headway at all toward recruiting participants.

I have come to the conclusion that we should refer to any plan that develops here with the coach as "mutiny." The Skipper has worked long and hard to retain nautical terminology here. Who are we to spoil the game? I must have slipped in "game" there because I am now using the word "coach" in place of bus. What a tangled web we weave, and we haven't really decided on the deception! Stick with me, though, folks. We'll get through this one way or another.

❧

Y ou probably have been puzzled by my references to "our" table at bingo. Like most of the other activities around these communities, we have almost a ritual for bingo, just as certain people play bridge together and some have their own group for shuffleboard. Most of the shuffleboard players seem to come from Ohio.

At bingo, we have sort of our own clique on Wednesday and Saturday nights. Not only our same bunch of players. We sit at the same table next to the same other players at their other same tables. You got it. They tell me during the first year of Snug Harbor one couple suggested they draw for bingo tables and bridge partners every week in order to get better acquainted with "our new neighbors." They don't live here any more. Nobody remembers their name. Rumor has it they went back to Topeka.

We do have an interesting little crowd. I'll introduce you. Of course, you have met Bess Ferguson, gym teacher. But did I tell you that Bess moved here with her sister? Yes. Bess's sister from Wyoming chose this place. She had been a widow about a year when she convinced Bess they should "drop anchor" here, as the Skipper puts it. Shortly after they were all settled in, one of the sister's neighbors from Wyoming appeared on their doorstep and it didn't take him long to convince the sister that Wyoming winters weren't all that bad with a man around the house. So Bess lives alone. She has never married and seems to enjoy her independence. Like I've told you already, that Bess is a wonder.

You know about the Colemans, Ruth and Emmett. After tonight's game and the coffee meeting planned at Bess's in the morning, they might give up bingo.

Have I mentioned Katherine Haley? She's a dear little lady from my home town, Colorado Springs. Her husband was a doctor, too. Katherine and I were never close friends back home. We knew each other, went to the same church, but since we've both been here I've become quite impressed with Katherine. She's no dummy. Just a tad bigger than Sister Anne. And she has a most charming manner. Quiet humor. Wears high heels and her hair in a French twist. I wear flats and my hair is twisted, Colorado style, on the back of my head. One thing about Katherine: she can be a real bore about her husband. Being married to a doctor was the biggest thing that ever happened to her, I suppose.

I never really knew Katherine's husband. He practiced at the "other hospital." You know how doctors are about such things. I do recall he had a dapper manner and a slight southern accent. Apparently Katherine didn't have any contact with his family, which seems strange. She has a picture of his ancestral home in Charleston of which she is very proud, but she's never been there. I don't understand that.

One other couple always plays with us, the Lannings. Remember I told you she sometimes wears an old fur coat because of the air conditioning? They're from Missouri and I'm pretty sure he was in politics. Not an office-holder like a senator or county commissioner — I see Howard more as an appointee. He must have served on highway commissions and liquor boards. I can give him first prize as "Mr. Regulatory Agency" because Howard can always quote chapter and verse on any civil matter. Like parking tickets and traffic violations. Howard tells old jokes in a loud voice and quotes Harry Truman a lot. I don't mind. Compared to some we've had lately, I like Harry Truman more every day.

Now, Howard's wife, Lorraine, bears watching. She is by far the most unpredictable of the regulars. One day she's sweet as can be, next time she might be a real — well, bitch. I'll need to know her better to write much in these journals. She looks okay. Her hair is frizzy blonde, her clothes made for someone twenty years younger, but she keeps her nails done and has a good complexion. I need to know Lorraine better, I guess.

Of course, there's George. You know him almost as well as I do, by now.

The last man on our "team" calls himself James Madden Wentworth. Tweedy type. Tall. And sort of mysterious — a loner. He lives in an apartment at one end of the Bridge. At first I assumed he was part of the staff, but he has no obvious official function. He walks around alone a lot, like he's on some sort of a health kick. Never goes near the pool or the shuffleboard courts. And here's the strangest part: I have never, ever, seen him leave the grounds. He eats all of his meals in the Captain's Mess. Plays bingo at our table. Goes to photography and some of the lectures. Sits at the bar and talks small talk with the men most of the day.

No — wait! I thought of something! Wentworth always buys the *New York Times* and the *Los Angeles Times* and he sits at a corner table in the bar half the day devouring those newspapers. Then he joins the conversation with the other men. Only after his papers. Howard Lanning kids him about that.

One more thing about Wentworth: He's not a bad-looking man. Tall, as I said. Interesting features. Sort of a Charleton Heston.

The Skipper watches him. Why did I just realize that? Whenever

Wentworth is in a lecture or game or class, the Skipper seems to drop in. Not at any other times.

At any rate Wentworth's an attractive, interesting man and seems to be eager to talk about the places he's been and the trips he's taken.

That's everyone. The cast of characters. And me, Lillian Morrison. I think I'm oldest, but not by much.

❧

We had our usual game tonight. Katherine won three dollars. Howard suggested we need more action around here and thought Bess could start a ladies' putting derby. I took my cue from George and Bess and led off a conversation about travel.

"Well, I enjoyed this bingo tonight," I started. "One of these days I'm going to win. On that third card I really thought I had it. Don't know why I'd even think of winning; I never have won bingo. John used to win a lot on cruise ships. He'd play bingo every afternoon, but I finally gave it up. I just loved the shipboard life and left the games to him. On our cruise through the Panama Canal he almost made our expenses at bingo and in the ship's casino."

"Oh, don't you just love the Panama Canal?" Lorraine Lanning had spent most of the evening waving her empty wine glass at a waitress and complaining about being cold. "Howard and I just loved the Panama Canal, didn't we?" Howard shrugged.

"It's interesting as far as the engineering is concerned, Mrs. Lanning." James Madden Wentworth was almost looking down his nose at her. "There's not much to be learned on a Canal cruise except for that one day of transit. I'd far rather spend my free time in cities where museums and libraries and special events are always going on. Give me Paris or London or Milano or even Rome. Have you been to the Tate in London? Or seen the Elgin Marbles at the British Museum? That's my idea of a worth-while trip."

Bess, right beside me, gave me a punch in the ribs. "Free time? What does he have besides free time?" I shrugged.

Ruth chimed in on cue. "You're right, Mr. Wentworth. I'd rather go someplace to learn something, too. Of course, with the chores on the farm and all, we never have had free time as you speak of, but I have a list a mile long of places I'd like to go and things I'd like to see. Beginning right here in our own country." Then Emmett shrugged.

Katherine Haley started in on her regular spiel about how much she wants to go to Charleston. "My dear husband took me wonderful places, but we never did get to his boyhood home in South Carolina." We had heard this many, many times before. "I don't know why he refused — Charleston must be a lovely town. On two rivers. I have kept a picture of —" At that point we all shrugged.

Just as if we had coached him, Howard chimed in about how awful airports are, and how it's such a pity the trains don't run like they used to. Lorraine got all worked up about losing luggage, but most of the night she spent trying to get a waitress to fill her wine glass.

Just about then Bess stood up, told everyone good night, and invited us all for coffee and sweet rolls in the morning. She's getting her ducks in a row, that Bess is. This project might work yet.

But I won't even be in the running unless I get some sleep. This staying up half the night trying to record what goes on at this place is more tiring than I thought it would be. So, 'til tomorrow at ten.

⌁

BLESS BESS

This morning reminds me of the dawning of my daughter's wed-ding day, or my own wedding day, or the morning of my first Coke date with John at the Canteen between classes, or any one of the days I faced piano recitals and still couldn't remember the second part of the third page of my piece, or sitting in those stands watching our sons play football or wrestle, or the day John would graduate from med school and we already had two kids and only the G. I. Bill, or the first morning of Rush Week — stomach tied in knots.

Today we will have coffee at Bess's casita and try to explain the bus (coach) plan to the rest of the group. As usual, I see the lights on at the Coleman's and over at Bess's.

George is up, too. Dear George. One rainy night he must have been feeling really down. He told me, "The worst part of every day is waking up and knowing Esther's not beside me. That's the worst part." Poor dear. Good thing it doesn't rain out here very much or George would really be a wreck.

As soon as I saw the Ferguson lights on, I called Bess to ask her what I could do to help with the coffee and sweet rolls. It really should be the Lanning's turn to have us all over, but Lorraine seemed out of it last night, so Bess invited us instead.

Probably better in her house where she can be hostess and sort of in charge, anyway. I did tell Bess I'd fix a fruit tray. That always adds color. We get together like this almost every Thursday morning. I can't recall how it got started, but now I think it's a good thing to have this routine. Nobody will be suspicious when we arrive at Bess's all at once.

Except the Skipper, of course. He usually cruises by in his golf cart shortly after Wentworth shows up. We're used to that. Even Howard Lanning has stopped commenting about Skipper being the warden.

Once Katherine Haley ran out in front of her cottage and invited the Skipper to come on in and join us. The Skipper muttered something about checking on the crabgrass and went putt-putting off in a hurry.

At any rate, we'll all be in Bess's living room in a couple of hours. I've been trying to think what I could say to add to the sales pitch, but not much comes to mind.

First, I'd better examine my own thoughts about this wacky deal. I have been known to go off half-cocked more than once. Just why do I want to get together with a bunch of old folks and travel around in a stolen bus? I never in my life chose to ride a bus when any other transportation was available. Now why would a sixty-nine-year-old widow who apparently still has good sense jump on a bus with a farmer and a nun and, for all I know, some kind of a crook? To see Mount Rushmore? To ride the ferry to Vancouver? To admire the arch in St. Louis? To make new friends in Minneapolis? Why? I'd better know before I get any deeper into this deal.

I hate to use the word, but I'd say boredom motivates me more than anything else here. This living the same life day after day, week after week, has its charms for a while. But I'm like the rest of this crowd. I've always been active. I've always been an achiever, even if the achievement didn't mean much to anybody but my family, or just to me.

The rest are the same. Emmett was proud of his corn crop. Bess took pride in the winning teams she coached. George never scratched a fender or missed a schedule.

Whoa, Lil! Back to the subject. I'll put it like this: We all need time away from here and conventional transportation does not meet our needs. Trains don't go where we might want to visit; planes are difficult and expensive. Charter bus trips cost a fortune if you want to get off the beaten path. We're too old for motorcycles and too smart for camping. I cannot get over the feeling, though, that we ought to do this together. Share the experience.

So here we are with a bus. We won't hurt the bus. We'll bring it back. If the Trailways people had been upset about the missing bus they could have sent someone to get it off the road. They've a lot of busses. I've seen those lots. The rolling stock is overwhelming. No wonder they can't keep track, or don't care.

Of course there's the matter of the nun. For starters we could all be of real help to that poor little waif if we'd just trim her shrubbery. But better still, we can give her a ride to upstate New York and find out what those sisters mean by leaving her all alone with those hungry cats.

Think of it this way: We're on a highway in Nebraska and a cop pulls us over. Who do we send out to talk to the nice policeman? You got it. And maybe Katherine Haley with her house picture.

We can put funds together share by share just like our lunch kitty. Bess will have some sort of guidelines, I'm sure. Bless Bess. This trip is tailor-made for her talents.

⤳

Well, I went over to Bess's coffee ready for some discussion and I certainly wasn't disappointed. You should have been there, but I'll tell it to you best I can. Words were flying thick and fast there for a while. I made some notes.

The Lannings arrived just after I did. I went early because of the fruit plate. Howard settled himself in Bess's grandfather's rocker. "I always like to come over here early, Miss Ferguson," Howard grunted, "before Coleman hogs the best chair in the place. Your grandfather must have been about my size."

Lorraine perched on one of the side chairs. Lorraine sits two ways. She either perches or she poses. I passed the fruit but she didn't want any.

Katherine Haley and George came soon after. Katherine was carrying a brown paper-wrapped parcel under her arm. "I brought the picture I told you about." She said that as if she hadn't already shown it to us at least a dozen times.

George had his sweater buttoned wrong. First time I'd seen that happen.

"Well, Mr. Lanning," George said as he took a seat at the end of the couch, "How's everything with you?"

"Just swell, George. Just peachy-keeno. Oh, my fingertips are getting calluses from shuffling cards for my solitaire games, but I'm thinking about getting some rubber gloves. Or maybe I'll just let Lorraine shuffle for me."

Lorraine shrugged. "All he ever does is play solitaire. Can you imagine that? He reads the paper, then out come the cards and he sits there half the day putting red sevens on black eights. Drives me crazy with that shuffling. You'd think . . ."

But nobody was listening. Instead, we had all turned our attention to Emmett and Ruth as they came in. Emmett stood around looking for all the world like the proverbial bastard at a family reunion. Ruth poured coffee for both of them and sat beside George. Emmett stood.

Last to appear was Wentworth. James Madden Wentworth. Only man I ever met who introduced himself by three names. Stage names, I think. He accepted the coffee and sweet roll with his usual good manners, then sat on the piano bench across the room from the rest of us.

Bess didn't waste any time. She stationed herself in front of her old walnut chest. She put on her schoolteacher voice, I thought.

"Something has come up that we need to discuss." She cleared her throat. "As a matter of fact, several of us here have a proposal to share with you. Just an outline or sketch of a proposal, actually, but we want to get some ideas from all of you. We've gotten pretty well acquainted at bingo and so forth, and feel that you who are here this morning make a good group, so Lillian Morrison and Ruth Coleman and George and I have sort of a plan. A germ of a plan."

She paused, but nobody spoke. "On Tuesday, Ruth and Lillian and I met a dear little nun whose bicycle had broken down. She lives in a fascinating old convent in Redlands. At the same time, George Schroeder just happened to be riding on a bus — a Trailways coach — that vapor-locked and died between Beaumont and Banning."

"Well, Miss Ferguson, I can see why you couldn't wait to share this excitement with the rest of us fun-loving bingo fanatics. Imagine! A nun and a bus the same day! And both broken down, so to speak. That's one for the Guinness Book."

Bless Bess. She laughed at Howard's remark and went right on. "We knew you'd be all worked up about it, Howard. But there's more to the story. In the first place, nobody from Trailways ever showed up to take care of the bus beside the road. So Ruth and Lillian and I helped George, as much as we could, to get the bus off the open road, so it wouldn't be destroyed by vandals. I'm sure you all know how much George cared about busses — coaches — during his career in Pennsylvania."

George blushed.

"Now, we found this barn where the man let us store the bus for fifty dollars a day." Emmett snorted, but Bess went right on talking. "But we had to move the vehicle out of that barn right away because the barn will be torn down to make way for a shopping mall. So we remembered that this dear little nun has a huge barn —"

Bess seemed almost out of breath. It was time for the co-conspirators to take some of the heat, so I interrupted. "In other words, what we four want you to know is that we have an abandoned bus in a nun's barn and we would like to know if any of you has some idea of what we might do — what use we might make — of this unusual set of circumstances."

The Lannings and Wentworth were open-mouthed. Katherine Haley had taken the wrapper off her picture.

Emmett had tuned up his roar. "Just one minute here. You say 'four of us.' Do you mean my wife? In on this idiocy? Oh, no, ladies! There might be three lunatics in this room, but not four. Not Ruth Coleman. You leave us out of this. I can see you're hatching up some big plan where you think you can talk this bunch of dummies here into going on some wild-hair trip around the country. You're thinking we're all dissatisfied with this place. You're probably planning some way to drive around the whole U S of A on a stolen bus without getting caught. Right? Wrong, lady. You are dead wrong. Not me. And not my wife. This place here is paid for and it's comfortable and we're not goin' any-place."

In the stunned silence Lorraine Lanning had come to life. "You all think we might take a trip together? A trip on this bus you found? Will the nun go along? I think that sounds like fun. Howard, we can go. Is the bus big enough so Howard can shuffle at the back of the bus where I don't have to hear him?"

"Lorraine, this bus — if it's a Trailways Landcruiser — is so big they won't even be able to get it into the police parking lot when we get arrested for grand larceny, among other small misdemeanors like operating a bus without a license and a dozen other miscellaneous charges."

"See, Ruth? You see? This is a stupid half-baked idea. Now let's go on home." But Emmett didn't move.

George stood up, looking straight at the front of Emmett's shirt. "Coleman, just calm down a minute. What we are suggesting makes sense. These ladies and I talked this over a lot. The vehicle is safe now, but we need to make some decisions. Last night after bingo you heard every one of us mention some sort of travel we have liked, places we have enjoyed. This is a chance for us to share some of those good times. I'd really be pleasured to see your farm in Iowa. Must be beautiful in the spring. And I'd love to see Kansas City, and where the Lannings lived, and maybe Old Faithful. Have you ever seen Old Faithful, Coleman? Have you ever seen Plymouth Rock, or New Orleans, or . . . We could all tell each other what we know about different places. I could show you about Pennsylvania Dutch country. I could even get you some scrapple and shoo-fly pie. We could have a good time, and here we have this bus!"

"*You* have a bus. I do not own a bus. I do not want a bus. I will not be part and parcel to any bus-stealing scheme —" Emmett again, of course. Now Ruth stood to face him.

"Emmett, I am sixty-nine years old. You are seventy-three. The drive out here to Snug Harbor was the first real trip you and I ever had together. We stayed at home on the farm and I spent most of the last few years taking care of my parents in town and your mother during the thirty years she lived with us. Now I am very much aware of what you and I have missed in our lives. If these good people can get this collective bus trip going, I don't care where we go or what we do or how much time we spend in jail. I am going along. Before I get any older or you get any more crippled with your arthritis, we owe it to ourselves to have this kind of a vacation. You can stay home and hoe your precious carrots if you want to, but I am going, and that's that!"

Emmett grumbled. "You always bring it down to your folks and my folks. You have to blame it on my mother. Good God, Ruth."

For the first time, and to our great relief, Emmett sat down and looked like he might keep his mouth shut.

Let me give credit where it's due here. During all that time Emmett was carrying on, the rest of us were thinking our own thoughts. He yelled about possibilities we hadn't even imagined. So I guess he really helped us make up our minds. Especially since he finally quit yelling. At least temporarily.

After her introductory remarks, you might say, Bess had not uttered a sound. She had been on the sidelines, watching the expressions on our faces. Now she had the floor.

"Well, you all have had some time to think this over. We could probably cover the territory we'd like in four or five weeks before returning the coach to Trailways."

"Returning the bus? We're going to give it back?" Lorraine fairly jumped up and down. "Why, Howard, that's not stealing, that's joy-riding. You can get us out of that. You always did before. Count us in, Bess. Howard can be the official ticket-fixer."

I won't try to describe Howard's expression.

Katherine Haley couldn't keep still. "Please! please! I'd love to be included, especially if we can go to Charleston. I feel like Ruth. I'm not getting any younger and I want to get things done while I can."

Bess shifted on her feet, sort of regaining her position as chairman, I'd say. "We haven't heard a word from you, Mr. Wentworth. How do you feel about all this? What do you have to say?"

"Interesting. I find this intensely interesting. And a challenge. I must say that in the years I was on the stage, I played in a great many mysteries. One primary consideration of any of those plots was the fact that the clues most often missed were the most obvious. The more easily spotted, the less often discovered. So I would suggest that the bus should be decorated in some way to advertise to all who see it that this bus belongs to a specific group of persons traveling together. In other words, we should masquerade this journey."

I thought this was a splendid concept, but count on Howard Lanning to smart off. "Just what group do you propose we go as, Wentworth? The graduating seniors from Waco, Texas? The Denver Broncos? Some new rock group?"

Now it was my turn to smart right back at Howard. "No." I said it as firmly as I could. "We should travel as the Golden Roamers Shuffle-board Club from Fort Lauderdale, Florida." That was all I needed to say about that.

For the first time in the three years I had known him, James Wentworth grinned at me. He has a beautiful smile.

"You got it, Lillian. Perfect." George was smiling at me too. "But there's one small hitch here. Who's gonna paint the coach? We can't just take some cans of enamel up to the barn . . ."

Silence.

Emmett stood up again. Oh, darn, I thought, here it all goes again. But Emmett had a different look. His voice was soft.

"You all know I am opposed to this — this whatever. You also know my wife wants very much to go along. She's my wife. So I'll go. And I do know where we can get the camouflage job done on this monstrous bus. And it shouldn't cost us one red cent."

Ruth stared. "Oh, Emmett, not Jake!"

"So why not Jake? He owes us plenty from all those years back in . . . Ruth's sister is married to a guy in San Bernardino who has a body shop where he appears to specialize in repairing and rebuilding race cars from Ontario and other tracks around. What he really is is a fence. He repaints stolen cars for resale. He can do this job. He can even get us the papers and the plates we need. We can also get him to restore the original colors when we get back. That's all I have to say."

"That's plenty, Emmett." Bess could not conceal her delight. "We have much, much more to discuss, but let's break this up right now. How about our usual Friday cocktail hour tomorrow? At Lillian Morrison's, I believe. Right now, head on out of here. That's the third time the Skipper has passed here in the last ten minutes."

❧

COOKERY AND CONVERSATION

The clock struck twelve just as I came in the door. Two hours. We had been "at it" for two hours. But I must say the time had been well spent. We each had made some sort of contribution, and even Emmett had come around, eventually. I fixed myself a quick lunch of cottage cheese and stuff, but I was almost too worked up to eat. Now for me, that's almost a record on the worked-up scale.

It took me most of the early afternoon to write the journal entry about the morning's conversation. I've checked it over. I don't think I left out much of real importance, but I did forget Howard Lanning's retort when Ruth said we'd all have a lot to talk about when we return from this trip we seem to be planning.

Howard spouted his usual sarcasm. "Sure, Ruth. We can compare notes about who had the cell with the best view." He is a funny man, although biting at times. Still, there's something likable about him.

I finished at my desk in time for the women's meeting at three. Sometimes I get the feeling those women all swarm to those things because they can shake their husbands for a while. That sounds mean. But the conversation surely would have lagged at our house if John and I had been cooped up in four rooms day after day. Married for better or worse, but not for lunch.

Just about the time I walked over to the meeting, I saw the Colemans' car pull out. Bess and George were in the back seat. As they passed me, George waved something out the window. Bus keys. Obviously the deal had been struck with the errant brother-in-law. Full speed ahead.

I waved back, sat through the meeting, and went home to my supper.

Preparing meals for one in these little galleys, as we are instructed to call them, can be a challenge or a threat. I often wondered how it would feel to cook for less than a harvest crew when we had a houseful of teenagers. Now I know.

I've read all these clever cookbooks about imaginative food for one. Some might make some sense, like having basic foods on hand to combine in various ways. But some of these home economists have spent too much time behind the old mayonnaise jar. I read one enchanting article describing how we can make our meals more attractive by adding clever garnishes.

The author's ideas should have been in something titled *See Jane Cook.* Faces on our cottage-cheese salad? Poke in a couple of raisins and a slice of pickled beet? Then add an ice cream cone hat, maybe? And clever carrot curls for a dear ruffled collar? I should skin my knuckles on the grater for this?

The genius in charge then suggests in her "eating alone" advice that I should invite a friend over. Great. I can put this creation in front of my seventy-year-old friend and say, "Open the barn door! Here comes the bus!" and jam a spoonful of cottage cheese in her startled face. That's life in the fast lane.

I've been alone too much lately.

Actually what I did have to build into some sort of a supper was what was left of one of those gourmet bean-soup affairs that lacked a little to taste just right. I had doctored those beans in that "soup" twice already. Added some fresh cilantro and one of those enormous cloves of garlic. Then came the old try-a-shot-of-Tabasco trick, which reminded me of the man I met years ago who claimed he and his wife had been married so long they were well into their second bottle of Tabasco. Didn't do a thing for the flavor, but it did cheer my day a bit.

To be brutally frank, I think some Heart Smart fanatic had used a fake salt in this gourmet mixture and there was no way of getting around that. Just my theory.

I also had half a chicken breast that had to be used, and part of a package of brown rice. Not a promise of a feast, but putting it all together would mean using only one pan.

Luck was with me. Just as I put the whole mess on low heat to congeal as best it could, Katherine Haley rang my doorbell. And just in time. I had my eye on a can of mushroom soup.

Katherine had her shrimpy dog, Sweetie, along. Sweetie groaned at me as I opened the screen door.

"Do come in, Katherine. I'm delighted to see you. Have you and Sweetie been enjoying your walk?"

"Oh, Lillian, you know Sweetie and I always have such a good time. Am I interrupting anything? I just — I wanted — I really felt I need to — well, talk to somebody about all this about the bus and all that. Can you explain more about the whole affair? I'm confused about the nun. Why would a nun have a bus? And I was astonished to hear Mr. Coleman so upset. He so rarely says anything, and then to have him start yelling like that! After we left, I sat a long time and tried to make some sense. But I did mean it about going to Charleston. Do you suppose this escapade could get me to Charleston after all these years?"

"Katherine, I am so sorry. Of course the whole mishmash this morning was confusing. I should have realized that. But we had to leave before the Skipper wondered what we might be up to. Now why don't you stay for a bite of supper with me, and we can go over the whole deal from the very start." As soon as I heard myself say that, I knew I was in trouble. Supper with me? With that skillet full of — well, I had said it.

"That would be lovely, Lillian. I haven't had much of a chance to visit with you lately. And whatever you have on the stove smells wonderful."

Little did she know. "Look, dear, I just threw some refrigerator remnants into a pot. You've probably never had such a combination."

Katherine has a warm high laugh. "Lillian, don't you know we all have suppers like that? The foods I put together just to clear out the Tupperware would never have passed inspection at our house. Some nights I try to trade for Sweetie's Alpo, even Steven. But Sweetie's too smart for that. Whatever you've concocted will suit me fine, especially if you have some ketchup."

❧

We sat at my miniscule kitchen table feeling more like real friends than we had even when we'd been living on the same block back in Colorado.

I told Katherine what I could about the proposition and the bus. She was particularly intrigued with Sister Anne, which surprised me a bit. Katherine and her husband had been veritable pillars of the enormous Methodist church smack in the center of Colorado Springs. She asked about the convent, about what the tiny nun could accomplish by going back to the Mother House. She wanted to know more about Mike, the old man who appeared to be the only helper Sister Anne had.

Through all this she ate that ghoulish goulash as if she had never before enjoyed such an excellent meal.

"You know, Lillian. Yours tastes a lot better than the stuff I throw together, but I think it's partly because I'm not eating it alone."

"You're right, Katherine. Let's start having more of our toss-pot suppers together. I'm ashamed I hadn't thought of it before." And I meant that.

"Nonsense, Lillian. Of course we can start sharing our suppers, but don't be ashamed. I could have thought of it just as well as you. I guess when we got here we just assumed everyone had their own way about things and wanted to be left alone."

Conversation drifted for a minute. I dished up what was left of some peanut-butter-flavor frozen yogurt and we went to the living room for our dessert. Katherine Haley closed her eyes as if deep in thought. "Lillian, I want to talk more about the Holy Sister. About her being included on this trip to wherever."

Good Lord, I thought, is this woman going to turn out to be prejudiced about Roman Catholics after all these years?

"Lillian, she must be subsisting on next to nothing up there. Where on earth would she find the money to pay her share of this trip? We said we'd all chip in so much in equal shares, didn't we? And she doesn't even have money enough to buy new candles for her little chapel? Well, I want to pay her way. I don't want her to know that, Lillian, but I want her to be able to go without worrying about her share. And I don't think the entire group should pay her expenses, either. She will be my financial responsibility, and that's that."

I just wanted to hug her. "Katherine, back in Colorado Springs I didn't know you were such a kind and generous lady."

"Back in Colorado Springs you hardly knew I was alive," she said, grinning. "But I'll tell you one — no, two — things more. I intend to purchase several of those hundred-pound sacks of cat food for our absence, and I would like to know if her handyman Mike will take Sweetie while I'm gone."

⁃ॐ

DETAILS, DETAILS

Friday. Folks, can only four full days have passed since I sat here moaning and groaning about the doldrums of being washed ashore at Snug Harbor? That morning, I felt more like a beached whale than anything else. I apologize. Even at my advanced age and stage of development I had no real idea how quickly conditions of life can change as if by chance. Or maybe I had no idea how little it takes to entertain this crowd.

Now I'm preparing to hostess our usual Friday "cocktail hour" with an entirely different outlook than I had contemplated last week when I realized my turn had come around again.

I had considered setting out some Pepperidge Farm Goldfish and a few carrots and celery strips with some lite ranch dressing. Maybe open a jar of mild cherry peppers or pour some Cheese Whiz on some Fritos to zap in the microwave like the grandkids do. But not now. This will be an honest-to-gosh party. I might even cook up a couple of artichokes and fix a curry dip. I might even make some of Franny Boyer's cheese puffs. I might even — whoa, Lillian!

Well, I am going off to the market before the regular Friday crowd gets there. The man generally has fine fresh shrimp ready for eating if I get there early enough. I could fix those tiny shrimp on the artichoke leaves with the seasoned cream cheese. Oh, for Pete's sake! Celebrate, old girl, but don't scare these people off with your frenzy! They'll decide you've gone 'round the bend and sneak off without you.

All last night I had crazy dreams about loads of people on busses, all going off cliffs or rolling down mountains. I also awakened several times thinking, I've got to remember that in the morning. One I do remember: We must be sure all of the folks on this trip have plenty of their prescription medicine along. I don't know what they might be taking, but they have to know those friendly pharmacists cannot fill California prescriptions in Arkansas or New Hampshire.

Funny thing: Just as I was writing that last sentence, my phone rang. It was Bess Ferguson. She is compiling a check list for departure, as she calls it, for distribution at this evening's gathering. No grass grows under that gal! She wanted to know if I had any ideas and I told her about the prescription drugs so now I don't have to worry about it any more. Except for my own gout stuff. I also suggested she leave a few blanks at the bottom for whatever might come up in our next group discussion.

There are some problems if we honestly need this project to be a secret. Oh, we can all leave our cars in that huge barn, so our neighbors won't decide we're lying helpless on the floor when they realize they haven't seen us for three weeks and come banging on the door. We'll make our getaway in the dark, of course.

"I'm going to bring papers and pencils for each person to suggest places to visit. Do you think they should tell us preferences as to motels and such? We need to straighten out as much as we can before we get stuck someplace with bothersome choices to make, don't you think so, Lillian?"

"You're full of good ideas this morning, Bess. I'll leave that to you. It has occurred to me the Skipper will wonder what we're doing with papers and pencils when he drives by. We can act like it's one of those word games like they play at Tupperware parties and bridal showers."

Bess laughed. "All we need is a bride. I've always been happy to have one real window on the front, instead of *all* portholes, but I'm beginning to see the Skipper's purpose. He can watch most of what goes on, can't he?"

"Well, until now we haven't been much fun to watch."

❧

I did manage to get myself under control about the cocktail party by the time I got to the market. Still, the food I served looked pretty splendid by our usual standards. Not the bill of fare at the Broadmoor, but better than we'd been doing.

Even Howard Lanning noticed. "Fine party here, Mrs. M., like a real celebration. Special occasion? Lorraine, you'd better have some of this food." Then he was off to snipe at Wentworth or Emmett again.

Bess brought out the paperwork after everyone had their drinks and a plate of something. Drinks are simple with this crowd. Wentworth drinks nothing but Budweiser. Most of the others prefer white wine. Emmett and I are the seltzer drinkers. Lorraine has a real taste for vodka. Sometimes she brings her own bottle. Often Howard has nothing at all.

My living room seems small, but with some of those folding tables around, nine people can be relatively comfortable. I put the tables around to write on, too. We all looked busy there for a while, and the conversation around the room had certainly taken a turn from last week. Last week we were all making small talk about the news, and discussing how rotten TV has become on Friday nights. Tonight I heard snatches of lively talk about the Blue Ridge Mountains and the Olympic Peninsula.

It's amazing to me how many good ideas can come from a group at one time. Wentworth suggested that we all pay ahead on our utility bills. "Establish a credit to cover the next month," he said. "That way nobody will come around threatening to turn off the power so the staff here might wonder where you have gone."

"Let somebody back home, someone you can trust, know what we are doing." This came from Ruth. "Tell a relative or good friend how often you'll check in, so no crises can get by while we are on the road. Also, you don't want someone calling the front desk searching for you."

More of that sort of helpful conversation went on. Katherine seemed much more relaxed. She even talked about Savannah as well as Charleston. Emmett had little to say, except he did announce that *he* had taken care of getting the coach repainted with the help of Wentworth (will wonders never cease?) who had provided sketches for the paint job, which should be just right.

Emmett also explained, while Howard stared at him, that a bus is qualified as a commercial vehicle only by the bus seats for the passengers. "By remodeling the inside, replacing regular seats with lounge chairs and recliners and tables and such, this vehicle will no longer be considered a — coach. More like a private van."

George gasped. I thought he might pass out right there.

"Don't worry, Schroeder. Jake can put all the seats back as they were when he repaints the outside. When and if we get back from this wild goose chase."

Lorraine squirmed a bit in her chair. Howard reached for her glass, but she grabbed it back. Lorraine looked at each of us around the room. "Now, you tell me when we are going and what sort of clothes we might need. I started to pack today but Howard said I was taking all the wrong things. He says we won't pack like we're going off to Las Vegas, which is all Howard ever really wants to do. Just tell me when and tell Howard how much money and you can just count on us Lannings, signed sealed and delivered."

❧

I was happy that someone had brought up the money. Nobody — nobody — has a successful shared travel experience without settling money matters before they ever leave the home place. I found that out when I tried traveling with some of my dear old friends before I decided to make a clean break of it. Break *for* it might be a better term.

I had known two of these women for years and thought I knew them well, but when it came right down to the bucks, particularly when we no longer had husbands to work out financial details in the way men can, we almost lost our friendships over choosing a place for lunch or spending an extra five dollars for better seats at the Santa Fe Opera. My, what a long sentence! But what an important subject for us; we scarcely knew each other more than to remember that Lorraine had to have a bingo card with "O63" on it, and Emmett raised fine tomatoes, and Ruth's date cookies were out of this world.

Bess suggested a three-day plan. That is, we would have "company funds" for meals and gas and group expenses three days at a time. Motel charges would be individual so we could use our own cards, of course. Only the Colemans and the Lannings would want double rooms. Then Bess suggested to Katherine, "Why don't we bunk together? I haven't had a roommate since my sister left. Besides, if we need too many single rooms, we might have trouble getting reservations on short notice."

That did it. Three doubles, four singles. So far, so good.

"We ought to put in at least a hundred bucks apiece for an emergency fund." Howard had spoken up. "Miss Ferguson, we ought to call you the 'ringleader.' You can hold that thousand dollars in escrow, so to speak, in case we do have some real problem. We've made a lot of jokes about being arrested, but let's be ready with cash just in case. None of us wants to sign over travelers checks to pay a fine or to pay for repairs on a stolen bus."

Howard thought a minute. "That counts the Sister. I suppose we could all cough up enough to pay her share of this."

Once again Howard had opened the right door. I stepped right up. "No need to be concerned with the expenses for Sister Anne. Her financial obligations with us are being assumed. By an anonymous benefactor, as you say, George."

George stood as if to leave. "This has been a lovely party, Lillian — Mrs. Morrison. I want to say something. In all my years of operating the Lancaster-Lebanon Line through Hershey and Annville and all those places I hope to show you some day soon, I always felt that bus riders are some of the nicest people on the face of the earth. Now, I hope you won't be offended, but I must say, you people are turning into bus riders."

Bless Bess.

LET'S GET THIS SHOW ON THE ROAD!

I did it! I finally did it! Saturday morning I dashed off to Palm Springs to the computer store and bought a word-processor, a dear little laptop Toshiba to take along on the trip. The clever young man even showed me a printer the size of a carton of cigarettes. I'll need that, too. And I'll tell you what made up my mind for me. It was the evening news after the gang left the cocktail hour at my house last night.

Right now I'm sitting here using this thing. The young man was most helpful and I've been messing around with it for a couple of hours. It's fun. Not nearly as complicated as I thought it might be. So now I am on the cutting edge — keeping right up there with any seventh grader west of any given point. A real member of the auto-mated age. Next thing you know, I'll find out about fax and all that.

But what about the newscast? How could that have persuaded me to get this machine?

There's this charming young man on the ten-o'clock news who has a real way about him. He seems to enjoy his job. So he's my favorite. Last night, he started to crack up when he read this item, and he caught my attention. (Often I have a tendency to doze through some TV.)

"Continental Trailways reports a bus has been stolen or lost. A bus has disappeared, apparently without a trace. Company spokesmen today announced that a Landcruiser last reported discharging passengers at Banning last Tuesday morning has not been seen or heard from since."

The newscaster started to laugh. "How can you lose a bus? What's bigger than one of those busses? Anyway" — he tried to smother his amusement, without much success — "Trailways people are asking if any of you folks out there" — he could hardly continue — "if any of you folks in the area spot a runaway or stolen bus, please call Trailways."

The kid was convulsed. "Did they leave an 800 number?" he called, apparently to the producer. "Should we try to apprehend the bus-hijackers ourselves or are they armed and dangerous?"

From off camera came a dry voice. "Just give us the news, bub." And they broke to commercial in a hurry.

So. Our bus had been missed. Police and other bus drivers, at least, will be looking for it.

Now we have a story here, folks. It's time to take this reportage of mine seriously. I'd better have this neatly typed because some day my manuscript might be introduced as evidence. Someday I might be interviewed by Joan Lunden as the keeper of the chronicles of the Golden Roamers Shuffleboard Club and Confidence Gang. MGM will want to make a mini-series. Maybe the story will read better if we have spent some time in the slammer. That could happen, I suppose, but as Katherine Haley says, "Who would give people our age more than ninety days?"

ﾟ

You won't believe this, but we are on our way. Just like that. Just one week after our Big Tuesday, we gathered at the convent at four-thirty this morning to be sure we got away before daylight. I've been too busy to write much since Saturday. Besides, it took longer than I thought to get this little machine under control. We understand each other, now.

At bingo on Saturday night I really worried that we might be attracting too much attention by having too much fun. We were all laughing and talking at once. Even Wentworth had a couple of jokes. One of the ladies at the next table told me he must be drunk. I just laughed, and that made them stare at us even more. Finally, Bess made a couple of cautionary remarks, like, "These people might have heard that newscast, too," and we kept our merriment to ourselves a little better. Bless Bess.

Sunday and Monday we must have behaved like whirling dervishes. Only one major group project remained, then our own packing and such. The group project came as a shock.

Just as we were saying good night in front of the Ship's Tavern after the bingo game (nobody won, but nobody cared), Howard Lanning said, in a most conspiratorial way, "Well, Miss Ferguson, I'm assuming you ladies have it all worked out how we are going to look like this shuffleboard team. You do have the equipment and the team uniforms and the instructions about how you play the damned game, haven't you? I know you must have that all worked out. Or is the good Sister in charge of that? Perhaps she can be the coach of our so-called championship team."

You could just as well have hit Bess in the face with a sockful of wet gravel. "Howard, thank you. I must admit it never occurred to me to need that paraphernalia. Of course. We can get to K-Mart tomorrow for shuffleboard sets. Maybe even a transportable roll-up court of some sort. But we will need uniforms. Heavens! How could I have overlooked such an important —"

Believe it or not, Howard patted her on the arm. "Settle down, Bess. You pick up one set, George and I will each get another so we have plenty without raising any suspicions. We'll have to have enough of those sticks and things along to provide for anyone who wants to challenge us along the way. Meanwhile, I'll get a bunch of T-shirts printed up in assorted sizes. We don't have a real logo, I guess, but I'll have 'em print a manatee on the front and the names on the backs. Florida — manatees. Sloppy but satisfying. I'll say I'm sending them to my friends in Florida for a joke. They'll believe it. Manatees."

And off he went into the night, leaving Bess there shaking her head.

Anyway, here we are. George and the Colemans went for the bus in the middle of the night and we met before dawn at the convent.

I honestly don't know if I can tell you enough about this paint job. Wentworth must have worked on stage sets at one time, because this is a real showpiece. Basically, the coach is gold and green. Long swooping lines along the sides, fancy intertwined letters "GRST" on the doors. And on each side are "records" of our "team." Hysterical to us, but impressive (we hope) to anyone we meet.

The team name runs in huge letters along the side, of course. Below in letters that must glow in the dark, it says:

TAMPA INVITATIONAL 1985
RUDY VALLEE PRO-AM 1986
LAWRENCE WELK REGIONAL 1986
MIXED SENIORS, ARKANSAS 1987
MARCO ISLAND DOUBLES 1988
DAYTONA MIXED DOUBLES 1989

CHALLENGES ACCEPTED

Wild, isn't it? Inside, the whole thing is unbelievable. Jake took out all the seats and put in recliners and one couch along the sides. In the back are two tables like diner cars with handsome chairs. Anyplace you sit you can see in every direction because the seats all swivel. The windows are tinted sort of dark so nobody can really see in. There's a bar, of course, and a refrigerator, and a rest room.

❧

Right now we must be just south of San Luis Obispo. Sister Anne and Katherine are on the couch, visiting as if they had known each other forever. Howard does have his cards out at the other table, and Ruth, Emmett, and Lorraine are each in the recliners. Emmett did grumble as much as he thought he had to, I guess. But now he's asleep. Bess is in the big chair immediately behind George in the driver's seat. George has his nameplate, GEORGE H. SCHROEDER, in the slot above his head, and his cap fits right in with the decor.

Ruth has been designated troop treasurer and she's trying to figure out how much money we'll need when we have to put gas in this buggy. I'm no help with any of that, so I sit here typing away, absolutely amazed that we have pulled this off. Bess and I agreed this morning: Even if we don't get any farther than Santa Barbara, we have had enough of a good time to make it worth it.

But Santa Barbara will be our lunch stop. Beyond that . . .

❧

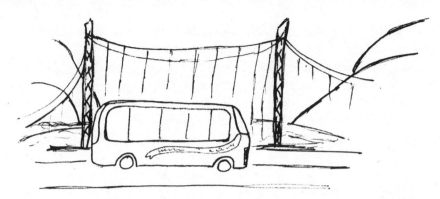

OPEN YOUR GOLDEN GATE, DAMMIT!

Beyond Santa Barbara, the fun began. That's for sure.

We found a great place for lunch, just what we hoped we'd find all along the way: a local restaurant with a good place to park the bus. Even out on the edge of town, a small crowd gathered, staring, when we got off.

"We might as well have a big sign saying 'STOLEN BUS,'" Bess remarked. Frankly, I felt pretty proud. Those wild colors really set us apart. Some onlookers even tried to peer inside, but George slammed the door shut right away.

We might have a small problem here with Lorraine. I say "small problem" because I am an incurable optimist. After all, we know these people only slightly, when you get right down to it. ·

That's one of the drawbacks to moving to a community like Snug Harbor. Nobody I know there ever met my husband — except Katherine Haley, of course. None of those folks ever watched my sons play football or were invited to my daughter's wedding. I have no idea how active they have been in their churches or whether they voted for JFK. I'm not about to discuss the Viet Nam War or the New Deal with any of them. We deal on a day-to-day acquaintance, with no basis in the core of our lives.

These friends could be likened to adding a sunroom on the back of the house or pulling a camping trailer — no real connection to the bulk of our lives. I digress, but that thought came to mind, especially after lunch today, because of Lorraine Lanning.

She's a wispy-looking woman. Doesn't seem brainless so much as semi-detached (like the sun room I mentioned.) About mid-morning I noticed she had a glass of orange juice, which she carried very carefully and kept right with her, even when she went into the lavatory on the bus. She seemed to be constantly rearranging the boxes of crackers and such in the cabinets under the bar.

Just as we started on the open road north from Santa Barbara, Lorraine jumped up and sort of shouted, "Oh, Miss Ferguson — Bess — I almost forgot something!" Bess looked startled, to say the least.

Then Lorraine headed for the front of the bus and picked up the microphone beside the driver's seat. She was carrying a yellow bowl meant for snacks and such, I guess, and she put the bowl in the empty chair beside her. Then she held on to George's shoulder and smiled this sugary grin and said:

"Welcome aboard, ladies and gentlemen. We are today's crew on your trip to San Francisco. George Schroeder — Captain Schroeder — and I are here to look after your safety and comfort."

Emmett sort of snorted and picked up his book. Lorraine went on.

"This coach, model 911, is equipped with three emergency exits. You'll find them clearly marked. Kindly look around the cabin to locate the exit nearest you." She waved her arms to one side and another, pointing.

Howard had stopped shuffling his solitaire cards. "Okay, Lorraine. Thanks."

Lorraine picked up the yellow bowl and held it in front of her chin. "Should there be any change in cabin pressure . . ." She put the bowl over her face, peering at Howard over the rim. I laughed. She did look funny. Bess snickered and Katherine watched as if she were seeing Lorraine for the first time. Jim Wentworth seemed more interested than anyone. "Kindly place the mask over your own nose and mouth before taking care of the small children."

Lorraine was on a roll now. "You will find safety instructions on the card on the back of the seat in front of you. May we remind you that regulations require all carry-on luggage to be stored completely under that seat in front of you during take-off and landing."

She jerked the cushion off the chair she was leaning on and waved it in the air, narrowly missing George's right ear. "This pillow is a flotation device in the unlikely event we should have an emergency landing over water." By now, even Emmett was laughing. Lorraine had become flirtatious, almost cute. "We shall begin beverage service shortly. The crew will appreciate it if you have exact change. The captain reports weather conditions are good, a fair tailwind with little turbulence expected. We should be landing just about on time."

Lorraine lurched to one side as George rounded a curve, but she regained her composure by leaning against Bess's chair. "Smoking is not permitted in the rest rooms. Tampering with the smoke detectors will —"

Howard applauded from his seat at the card table. "That's fine, Lorraine."

The rest of us applauded, too. Ruth and I had been laughing.

Sister Anne leaned toward Katherine. "What was that all about? How nice of Mrs. Lanning to be so concerned for our safety."

Jim Wentworth was sitting next to me on the couch. "There's more to Lorraine than we have seen at the bingo games," I commented. He just nodded.

Lorraine returned to the bar to put away the yellow dish. "Well, you had 'em rolling in the aisles. Funny girl." Howard said it loud enough for all of us to hear.

"You're not the only one in our family who can get a laugh, you know, Howard," Lorraine said. She sat down and kicked off her shoes.

We were beginning to settle in, I felt. Jim went forward to stand beside George. "How do you like this modification, Schroeder? Does the bus seem desecrated to you? After all your years, you must have a real appreciation for such a vehicle as this. Changing the seats around and all that . . ."

"Oh, I felt pretty bad about it 'til I got to thinking how comfortable this will be for all of us, and what a fine way to see eastern Pennsylvania when we get there. Best of all, she can all be put back right. I saw the seats all stacked up neat. But it did worry me at first, like a hex, maybe."

Jim looked at a sign along the road. "Salinas, huh?"

"Ever been there? My son has in-laws there, but I've never —"

"Only once." Wentworth smiled. "I had a buddy whose grandmother lived in Salinas. He hated the place and complained every time he had to visit there. One day I told him I'd been to Salinas, and he was surprised. 'I didn't know your grandmother lived there, too,' he said." Both men laughed. So did the rest of us.

Katherine Haley said, "How nice of your friend to visit his grandmother. I never knew any of my husband's family. You see, he never . . ." Her voice trailed off.

Sister Anne patted Katherine's hand, then peered up at Jim. "That's very funny. 'I didn't know your grandmother lived in Salinas, too.' You have clever friends, Mr. Wentworth."

"Some were much more clever than others, Sister. Please, call me Jim. We're all friends here, now."

Bess and I had been watching and listening. I tried to read her expression, but she made it easier. "Not even one day out and he's much more relaxed than I ever noticed at Snug Harbor."

꙰

When we made our first stop for diesel, Emmett started acting normal. I knew he couldn't go a whole day without making some kind of a fuss.

"Well, Schroeder, here's where your old trail ends. These guys are going to demand to know who owns this crate and want to see all the papers and all that. We're gonna' find out right here that those faked-up registrations and such Jake got for us aren't worth a shuck. Off to the clinker, Schroeder. Get set."

Ruth glared at her husband. "Not as long as we pay cash, Emmett. Just watch."

You know what? Ruth was right. The men made all sorts of comments about rich shuffleboard players, but nobody asked about anything. What did they care? We just look like a bunch of old fools on an old fools' outing. No questions there. I figure as long as we keep grinning, we'll get by.

The station attendants did show more interest than we expected, but that was mostly questions like, "how long you folks been on the road?" or, "playin' a lot of shuffleboard around here?" As long as only one of us answers, we'll be fine.

One other customer did show a lot of interest in our "team record" painted on the side. "You folks must be headed for Lakeside."

Howard had appointed himself the coach of our team, so we agreed to let him field the athletic conversations. He nodded at the stranger. "Where else?" he replied, grinning.

Poem of the day:

> My verse becomes more lyrical;
> There's been a minor miracle!
> Dear George has commandeered a bus.
> Now we're heading toward the Bay —
> We are truly on our way!
> Life has made a big right turn for us.

Amazing how much we are learning about each other, even on this first day. Bess sat down across from me as we approached San Francisco. "I have always loved this city. I loved to watch the fleet coming in and out during the two years I was in the Navy here. Always such a grand welcome."

I didn't know she'd been in the Navy. My only connection from younger days to San Francisco had been listening to radio. *One Man's Family.* We used to listen faithfully to the stories of the Barbour family. They lived at Sea Cliff. One of these days I'd like to see Sea Cliff, but not on this bus.

Just as I was immersed in those thoughts of the Barbours, Howard Lanning sighed.

"Ah, Fanny."

Well, I'm not the only Barbour fan aboard. Father Barbour had to say, "Ah, Fanny" at least four times on each broadcast, I'd guess. One more common ground. I'll let it slide now and bring it up in some duller moment, at dinner or somewhere. No use wearing out our entire repertoire in one day.

Bess had her clipboard and maps in her lap. She was sitting right behind George. "Next exit for the Holiday Inn, Captain,"

"Ain't it so, Commander." George saluted. And here we are.

~

Day number two. On the road. Yesterday I wrote bit by bit as we drove along. After today's events, I'm not sure what will be the best method of journalizing, but I'll tell you this: Many more days like this one and I'll need several more reams of paper for Toshiba and me. I'm tucked into the motel here at Reno now. This has been quite a day.

At breakfast, Bess announced, "It seems to me only fair that several of us should share the driving. If you all agree, our Captain Schroeder suggests we locate a suitable parking lot or other training field. Those of us who wish to be checked out as drivers — operators — can take his course. Any of you who do not relish piloting such a craft will practice shuffleboard at the same time."

That seemed like a good-enough idea. George had spotted a huge parking lot near some sort of a stadium where no traffic would interfere with lessons, so we put the plan into action. Now, I don't mind driving. I love my little car. But the prospect of having to park that big lug of a bus scared me off.

Sister Anne, Katherine, and I unloaded the shuffleboard stuff and started shoving the disks around one corner of the lot while the others drove enormous figure-eights and all that. Squealing brakes and screeching tires gave way gradually to smoother starts and stops. Our Golden Roamers chariot looked and sounded fine as first Howard, then Jim, then Bess, drove past us and waved. Chalk up one more for Women's Lib.

Sirens! The screech of sirens coming up the road to this lot nearly split our ears. Two police cars roared across in front of us toward our gleaming coach. The three of us froze.

George stopped the bus and was on the ground beside it before the young cops were out of their cars. They couldn't have been fifty feet from our "practice" spot, but we couldn't hear because they were on the other side of the bus. I rushed Sister and Katherine around to be in plain sight of the policemen. Seemed a good idea for them to know we had such a sweet-faced old lady and a nun aboard. Later, Bess laughed and complimented me on such a smooth move. Sister Anne impresses cops a lot.

George had his operator's license in his hand. "Something wrong here, officers?"

"You bet there's something wrong here, mister! We had reports of this big bus gyrating around this lot. Neighbors on the far side complained about the noise. What's the big idea? You can't bring an enormous vehicle up here to this lot and drive around in circles! Where's your operator's license? This don't belong on the passenger car lot. You can park it over there if you need to, but you sure as hell can't go making such a racket and tearing up this lot! This lot's closed on weekdays, anyhow."

"Officers" — George had his entire entourage lined up around him now — "officers, in the first place, this vehicle has been modified for private use and does not qualify as a commercial vehicle. We'll be happy to show you the inside if you need to verify that. The reason we're here is public safety, however." The young cops stared.

"I realized this morning" — George was offering his license for inspection as he spoke — "the brakes seemed to be slipping a bit. Now, you have a beautiful city here but the hills are a real challenge for any driver. I felt the brakes needed to be tested someplace where we ran no chance of causing injury or damage to another vehicle. So we came up here. Mr. Coleman, here" — Emmett turned a strange shade of purple — "Mr. Coleman here is an A-number-one mechanic and he has worked on these brakes for us a bit — just needed a little — and I do believe we're all set to get on our way to Reno, so we'll be on our way."

One of the policemen, the baby-faced one, shook his head. "That's really thoughtful of you folks to pull off the street to make sure your bus brakes are okay."

He had been studying the "tournament record" on the side. "You all played in the Lawrence Welk Invitational? Boy, would my grandmother love to meet you! She plays shuffleboard all the time. One year she went all the way to Lakeside. Shuffleboard and bingo. And does she love Lawrence Welk! You must be a really good team to go traveling around like this. Grandma plays on Tuesdays and Thursdays down by the Marina —"

Howard stepped up. "Howard Lanning, son. I'm the coach of these fine players. We'd certainly enjoy meeting your grandmother, maybe even arranging a match here in Frisco, but we have our schedule to keep. Now that Coleman has the brakes fixed we've got to hightail it to Reno. Big match there this week at the senior center. We really look forward to those Nevada shuffleboard get-togethers. We can make enough on the side in Nevada to pay our expenses the rest of the way, so we gotta get going. Okay if we load up and head on out now?"

The officers exchanged glances that looked to me more like sneers and walked away. "Guess you're okay if you don't make any more racket cruising around up here." Then off they went.

꙰

After one more ceremonial "shot" (I just loved watching Sister shoving that disk around with her stick — whatever it's called) we were pronounced ready to move along. We'd make one quick swing across the bridges and such, then on toward Reno. Ruth was helping Katherine load the shuffleboard equipment in the baggage storage place while Howard supervised.

A tangled thicket of heavy shrubbery lined the lot at that edge. Ruth was just ready to close the compartment when she stopped and turned toward the bushes.

"Come on, Ruth. You're holding up the whole trip. Whatever —?" Emmett just has to scold, I guess, but this made me cross. I was standing right there. So was Bess.

"I heard something." Ruth held up one hand. "Just then I heard something like a groan. Right near here. Do you hear it, Bess? Sort of moaning — in the bushes, maybe."

Ruth was walking toward the thicket. She looked pretty spiffy in her bright cotton print with blue flats to match, but she pushed right into those tangles like she had on jeans and a sweatshirt.

"Ruth! Wait a minute!" Bess was right behind her. "I hear something, too. Over this way, I think."

I followed close enough to see what happened. Then Bess exclaimed, "Over here! Here's a boy over here!"

I could see Bess leaning over what appeared to be a red sweater on the ground. Ruth pushed through the dead branches. George and Wentworth had followed them into a small clearing. Bess had turned the kid on his back. We could all make out what was going on now. She patted the youngster's hand and face.

"Oh dear." Katherine Haley stood beside me. "Is he dead? Is that poor child dead?" She raised her voice. "Ruth, Bess, is that poor child — dead?"

Bess had her hand on his wrist, then on his throat. "No, dear, he's just unconscious."

"Unconscious?" Lorraine had been the last out of the bus. She had her orange juice. "Would he like some juice?" Howard glared at Lorraine. I thought he was about to tell her to get back on the bus.

Ruth began to rub the boy's hands when a scream came from deeper in the woods. Two older boys came tumbling toward Ruth and Bess, who were on their knees beside the unconscious one.

"*Don't touch my brother!* Get away from my brother, you lousy old bags! Get away from him! You got no business, you old hags! Stay away, all you old sonsabitches!" His high-pitched voice was hysterical. This kid has the shakes, I thought — and I'd never even seen a kid with the shakes before.

Another, less hysterical, voice came, then.

"Hey, look, Tony! Those nice people found your baby brother, Tony. Just like Baby Moses, huh, Tony? What you gonna tell your mamma, Tony, about these dumbass old broads found your baby brother passed out at the park? Cute, man, cute."

The two older boys had come close enough that we could see them now. They were an absolute mess. I know they hadn't had clean clothes in days. Their hair was long and tangled with dead leaves and twigs all over. Their eyes seemed glassy. They lurched more than they walked. The screamer kept his arms out like he was trying to lean on something. This was a pair of dirty bums.

Bess didn't move. Neither did Ruth, but the two men, George and

Jim, stepped into full view of the renegades in the clearing. The taller boy wiped his filthy hand across his mouth, drooling. He ran his fingers over his matted hair, then hung one arm over the other kid's shoulders, swaying. Then he kicked at the boy on the ground. "That's Rafe down there, Tony. That's li'l ole Rafe. How you think, Tony? Rafe looks pretty good there, huh?"

"Aw, Gino, you asshole, cut it out!" He had started to cry. "What we gonna do? What if Rafe . . . ?"

"Conks out? What if your baby brother —?"

Bess stood facing these two hoodlums. "What's the matter with this boy? What do you two know about this?"

Gino pushed Tony aside. "Rafe don't need no help from you, lady. He needs to sleep it off. He'll be okay. Just got more than he could handle. Me and Tony can take care of him. You turkeys get out of here. You old farts just mosey on in your fancy bus. Me and Tony, we —"

Now Wentworth took over. "Listen, you bastard." Gino jumped as if shot. "Miss Ferguson here has determined this kid has no pulse to speak of, his eyes are rolled back — the kid is damn near goners. You better tell her just what this kid has taken, and we're gonna get him some help. You worthless punks shape up here and help this kid and this woman or we'll —"

The bigger kid had straightened up. He took one step toward Jim and lunged at him, kicking and punching and yelling all at once. "Get the hell out of here, you old goats! Just get out of here! We got enough trouble without you old goons hornin' in."

George — little old George — pinned Gino's arms behind him and held on. Wentworth shook his head. George spoke right into Gino's ear.

"What kind of dope did this kid have? Come on, now! This lady knows all about kids and dope. She can help this boy, but we must know what kind of stuff you guys gave him. There are two other men here besides us. You can't whip us all, even if we are old. So just settle down here, you jerks, and tell Miss Ferguson what she needs to know to save this kid's life!"

"Coke."

"Anything else?" Bess's voice sent shivers down my spine.

Tony, the brother, started to cry again. "He didn't come down. I tried to bring him down. I gave him a soaper. All I had, finally. Then he went like this."

Ruth looked around. "What's a soaper?"

Bess shrugged. "That's a new one on me."

"Quaalude." Wentworth almost whispered it. "The kid has had cocaine and Quaalude. Let's get him out of here."

"Those cops would leave right when they could be the most help," Bess sighed. "Well, let's put him on the bus." She stood back so the men could —

"Now, just one minute here, Commander Ferguson. You are suggesting we can put that dirty bum kid on our bus and go driving right up to the hospital with a dopehead? We are on a contraband bus trying to start off on a nice trip, and you want to expose us to possible arrest ourselves by playing Good Samaritan for some dumb kid who's not worth —" Howard sputtered. His face was crimson. He had his fists clenched.

Oh nuts, I thought. Now old Lanning is going to cause more trouble. I should have had more faith in Bess Ferguson's good sense.

"Mr. Lanning, would you like to stay right here with these other hoodlums while the rest of us take this youngster to the hospital? There is no need for you — or your wife — to go along and be caught delivering this boy in what we hope will be a life-saving emergency trip. Perhaps you could just find a cab and meet us at Fisherman's Wharf or some such. But this boy needs help. We are the only help for him."

And Bess strode toward the bus with Wentworth close behind, carrying one small limp body. The rest of us filed on. Howard and Lorraine brought up the rear, Howard muttering about "somebody's going to have to sign some papers to get this no-good admitted!"

Bless Bess.

❧

Well, it's late and I want to get on to bed or I might miss the bus in the morning if I oversleep. Nobody asked us anything when we got to the hospital, of course, and we made it here to Reno in fine time, but Howard pouted all the way, and Lorraine stuck to the orange juice.

❧

GEEZERS AND GEYSERS

Day five. Somewhere between Salt Lake City and Yellowstone Park. How do you like that for a dateline? Captain Schroeder and Commander Ferguson have rigged up a clipboard with maps and mileage and such for us to refer to as we go. That's fun.

First day, Palm Springs to San Francisco.

Second day, San Francisco to Reno.

Third day, Reno to Wells, Nevada

Fourth day: Salt Lake City.

Next stop: Yellowstone.

Oh, it's a bit cold this early in the season, but we avoid the crowds that way and enjoy off-season rates. I'll tell you one thing: We haven't spent much time fooling around in parking lots with our shuffleboard "practice."

Now, I have not much to add to this journal from Nevada. We played the slots at lunch in Reno. Jim Wentworth had some sort of a flu bug that day so he stayed on the bus. Didn't even get off for lunch. I thought that odd, since he has been so much more relaxed on this trip. Who knows? Suddenly he turned almost as withdrawn as he had been back at Snug Harbor. Just sat in the very back seat and waited for the rest of us. Katherine bought him some Budweiser. That made him feel a bit better; at least he smiled.

Salt Lake City I have seen before and I consider it one of the more interesting cities around. At least Salt Lake has maintained its own image and stuck to its original plan. Some of the group wanted to see the ski resorts just east of town, but Katherine had this look in her eye that morning. I knew she wanted to do something else.

"Katherine, what attracts you the most here in Salt Lake?" The least I could do was ask.

"Oh, Lillian, you'll think it's just the same old thing I'm forever fussing about. Here in Salt Lake the Mormons have the most complete genealogical records of anyplace in the country."

"I know that, Katherine. Did you by any chance think they might have some information you could use about the Haley family? Would you like to spend our day there in the genealogical library? If so, I'll be most happy to stay here with you. I have no burning desire to see Park City. My grandkids love it, but ski hangouts don't excite me."

"Oh, dear Lillian, do you wish you could ski?"

"No, Katherine, I just wish I could fit into the outfits."

She laughed, tiny size ten that she must be. I was happy to amuse her, I guess.

Anyway, the two of us went to the Family History Library. One personable young woman about Katherine's size almost adopted the old lady (notice that I call Katherine "old?") and spent a great deal of time showing her how to locate records from South Carolina in the stacks and on the microfilm. Not knowing much about such things, I found it to be a most interesting day. I do think they could find anyone's ancestors with bare-bones clues.

As far as Haleys in Charleston were concerned, there was no trace of one Edward Haley, in spite of Katherine's insistence. This young lady and Katherine did find some Haleys, but the line ran out with one Mary Lucinda Haley, whose married name was Grafton. Might have been a cousin, we decided, but no Edward Haley could be discovered in all of South Carolina. Interesting details.

We wandered on over to listen to the organ in the auditorium of the Tabernacle, but Katherine could hardly have been pleased with the day. Besides, the weather had turned cold and spitting rain. We loved getting back on our nice warm bus.

Speaking of rain, have I mentioned our weather reports? We have worked ourselves into quite a team on this trip, and have only been on the road four full days. Sister Anne prays to commence our opening exercises. Nice. Each morning George takes the microphone and details for us the itinerary for the day. He studies the Mobil Guides to alert us about the high points along the way. Then I am expected to brief the group on general news, headline stuff they might have missed. Jim Wentworth then adds special in-depth news from his newspapers, the *L. A.* and *New York Times* as long as he can get them. He has a real gift of gab and a remarkable fund of knowledge of background and such. Surprising man.

Bess comes on the mike next asking suggestions and preferences for the day's meals and motel, and such. She goes into detail of next-day expectations and all that. Howard Lanning gives a sports report about any news that catches his fancy. Lorraine tries to tell us a daily joke or funny story. So far so good. Ruth prepares a brief financial report and then (get this) Emmett volunteered to add a weather report, giving us the weather not only where we are but where we've been and where we're going. Katherine winds it all up with a favorite hint or recipe for motel-room cookery.

Yesterday Katherine shared one of her favorite hints — declared she learned it traveling with her husband: Every night she claims she put six prunes in a water glass and fills the glass with vodka. The next morning she throws away the prunes . . .

We all laughed when she told us, knowing it was her idea of a joke, but I'm not sure it shouldn't have been one of Lorraine's jokes. Whoa, Lil! With Lorraine, that wouldn't be a joke.

Three hundred and sixty-six miles, Salt Lake to Yellowstone. That's a good day's drive for us. We're all comfortable. Drivers change every two hundred miles or so. Our seating still varies, although a definite pattern develops as we go. Almost every one of us manages to snooze some in the afternoon. Bess reads a lot and so do some of the rest of us, so we have a basket on the bar for exchange of paperback books. Dick Francis ranks top of our best-seller list right now. Along with some golden oldies. Oh, we do have music, but only two hours a day. We each get an hour to play our own tapes throughout the trip. Bess has worked all of this out.

One other detail of our lives has worked out: We seem to be more casual in our dress. This morning George showed up with the first en-route T-shirt: Park City, Utah. Deliver me!

Grand Teton National Park lies just south of Yellowstone. Those mountains took our breath away as we approached. We're staying at Grand Teton Lodge tonight. So tomorrow's journal entry will begin after Yellowstone. Old Faithful, here we come! Our weather man, Coleman, says tomorrow will be unseasonably warm. The winter has been mild, anyway, so we are looking forward to a Golden Geyser Day.

❧

Just last night I was struck by the thought I might not have much to say from here on in this journal. I mean, in Salt Lake we couldn't locate

Ed Haley and we surely don't hope to take on any more kids all doped up. Actually, our bus does attract attention, but mostly admiration and numerous comments about Lakeside. Where in the world is Lakeside?

You should have been with us today. One more Kodak moment, as our sons used to say.

Yellowstone in off-season gives the visitor a real sense of the size of the park. After driving past huge expanses of grasslands and forests, some still basically burned out since 'eighty-nine, we found Old Faithful and the enormous old hotel there beside it. The few tourists in the park seemed to have congregated right there, even though the hotel was still closed. Mounds of dirty snow outlined the parking lots. The sun shone, however, and the color of the sky had all of us searching for new superlatives for blue or for brilliance.

Wentworth drove from Grand Teton. Approaching Old Faithful he remarked to Bess, "That sign says we'll have a forty-minute wait until the geyser does its thing again. Would you like me to pull up here by the covered drive in front of this grand old hotel so we can put on a little practice session? Might do well to reinforce the image, once in a while."

Bess, still mindful of Howard's biting criticism of the hospital side trip, simply smiled and passed the buck.

"Why don't you ask the coach? Sounds fine to me. I rather like shuffleboard, even though I know next to nothing about it."

Howard glanced up from his solitaire game. "Sure. Let's have a go. Lillian, you and Coleman play red. Ruth, you and George play black. I'll act as the official."

Of course you will, Howard, I thought. Of course.

That elegant hotel must be one of the biggest log structures in the world. In my world, anyway. We couldn't get in, which disappointed all of us. The staircases, fireplaces, and the rest of the decor overwhelm the visitors. The wide covered drive in front was just right for an early spring warm-up game. Other tourists awaiting the eruption of Old Faithful wandered around the snow-plowed drives and parking lots. During summer they would have been in the hotel or the bar or the shops near by, but today they simply waited. And shivered a bit.

Howard stood at "center court" of our portable roll-out linoleum shuffleboard "playing surface" spread on the drive. He had his Fort Lauderdale cap on, and a coach's sweatshirt complete with a fat gray manatee on the front. (What can be less attractive than a manatee?) The four of us chosen to play wore team T-shirts.

Even in an extra large, I shy away from T-shirts, but who did we know here? Who cared that Lillian Morrison felt she was embroiled in her own impersonation of a manatee in this get-up? Just the same, I was glad we were off-season. George and Ruth looked cute. Emmett and I looked awful. He had his T-shirt on over his zip-up jacket. Imagine.

Howard could not let well enough alone. He had a whistle. The minute he started tooting that thing this bored herd of tourists headed in our direction. I tried the best I could to get that disk to go in the right direction. We all did. Howard barked at us.

"Okay now, George, how do you expect to win at Omaha if you can't shoot any straighter than that?" Then, "Ruth, you're a little better on the lob shots, but let's get more work on that straight-ahead boomer."

Bess was standing behind me. "Do shuffleboard players talk about 'lobs' and 'boomers' back at Snug Harbor?"

"Don't ask me, Bess. All I know about this game is it's half-way home on my two-mile walk."

Emmett had turned that funny purple again. Ruth looked like she might faint. "Defense! Defense!" Howard was screaming. And blowing his whistle. I just leaned on that stick, whatever it's called, and waited for George to shoot my red one off the ten spot. He did, which necessitated several more bursts on the whistle and cheers from the gathering crowd.

Over near the doors of the hotel, standing up on a step to get a better view of this fiasco, a man about our age watched intently. A cute little boy about four years old clutched the old man's hand. Finally the man picked the child up to sit on his shoulders.

"I want to see the Faithful blow up, Grampa. I don't like snuffleboard."

"Okay, okay, Jimmy. We'll just watch this a minute. I think I'd like to . . ." As he said that, the man edged closer to us through the crowd.

Now, by Yellowstone standards, this was not much of a crowd, but when they all gathered under that century-old *porte-cochere* we knew how it feels to be one of the Final Four at the NCAA tournament. No sooner did Howard quiet down from his "coaching" us than spectators began shouting advice and encouragement. I must admit, some hecklers had a field day, too. And the man with the kid, after studying our bus carefully, tapped Howard on the shoulder.

"That your bus over there?"

"Yes, sir! It certainly is! We're a championship team from ––" Now Howard, I thought, why did you have to say that? Why don't you just shut up, Howard? But no. Howard was having the time of his life. "You people get right on with that practice. Can't let down a minute." So we kept at it, whatever it was we were attempting to do.

"I notice that challenge sign."

Howard could not have been more stunned if we had hit him with our sticks up the side of his head.

"Sign on your big fancy bus reads 'challenges accepted.' That a fact?"

Howard gulped pretty hard. "Well, that means team challenges. Not just one-man challenges."

"You mean you don't play singles, only doubles? That's a helluva shuffleboard team, can't play singles! I'm just waitin' around here for that geyser blow-off. Mister, I've played at Lakeside. I think I can beat any man or woman on your team and I got a fiver says I can prove it. Now what do you say to that, coach?"

"Well, if you've played at Lakeside . . ."

"Of course I've played at Lakeside! Me and the missus spend every July at Lakeside. After all, if you're really a shuffleboard player, how can you miss Lakeside?"

Howard just nodded.

Bess nudged me again. "Do we know about Lakeside? Like, what state it's in?"

I just laughed. "I have no idea. Poor Howard can't ask or the guy will catch on to what phonies we are." I looked at that stick I was holding. "He can probably tell, anyway, if he's such a whiz at the game."

By now, the whiz had put the child down on the drive and was unbuttoning his lumberjack coat. He pushed back his McCoy cap and waited for Howard to respond. Howard looked around, silently asking advice from Bess or whoever he could find. Needless to say, George and Ruth and Emmett and I had stopped. Dead still.

Bless his heart, Jim Wentworth stepped up, took my stick, and faced the challenger.

"Mister, we're a championship team and we seldom take on rank amateurs, but if you insist, I'll play you two out of three, just for the honor of our team. Keep your fiver in your pocket."

I leaned toward Jim. "Two out of three *what?*" I whispered.

Jim grinned. "Hell, how should I know? He'll keep score. I'll just nod along. Game seems simple enough."

The child at his side pulled on the man's sleeve. "No, Grampa, *no!*

Not more shuffleboard! That's all you ever want to do, Grampa. This ain't Lakeside now, Grampa. The Faithful is gonna—"

"Honey, we have lots of time. Plenty of time for me to clean this guy's plow. Go find your grandma." He turned toward the crowd. "Emma! Emma! Come get this kid!"

Emmett stripped off his T-shirt, thank heaven, and handed it to Wentworth. Ruth and George and I stood lined up along the side, feeling like absolute fools. Still, we had to stick with our teammate. We had to cheer.

The stranger won the first match handily, but in the second it was obvious Jim had figured out how this was supposed to work. He appeared to be ahead when I heard a voice behind me.

"I've got five'll get you ten the old man whips him two straight."

Another strange voice: "You're on, buddy."

The crowd behind me was stirring. I realized to my horror that money was changing hands. Some guy in one of those molded gray flannel caps from Brooks Brothers was making book on this sporting event. Bess rushed into the crowd, her hands above her head saying something I couldn't hear.

Nobody else could hear her either, because just at that moment a great roar came from over on the other side of the drive. People shrieked. Steam and roaring geyser filled the air. A small child cried, "Grandpa!" Jim Wentworth took advantage of the general confusion and knocked all those red disks clear to kingdom come.

That might have ended the whole affair if the park police had not arrived on the scene, having been alerted by a touring Baptist preacher to the fact that gambling was going on at Old Faithful. Their official-looking dark green truck, which could have been a paddy wagon, wheeled into the lot. Jim forfeited the third game, saying he had broken whatever that stick is. We all hightailed it back to our splendid coach, leaving Bess and Howard to work things out the best they could. Bless Bess.

We'll get a closer look at Old Faithful next time. When the park isn't so crowded. Right now, we're here at Buffalo, Wyoming. Next stops: Rapid City, Omaha, and Des Moines.

⮜

"WERE YOU SCARED, MOMMY?"

I did not think up this trip. Except for naming our shuffleboard team and all that, I have had very little to do with getting this show on the road. But I can tell you this: The entire project couldn't have been timed better or worked better than it has so far.

I don't want to jinx us, but we've had smooth sailing (as the Skipper would say) for seven days now. One whole week. And we are all the way into our seventh state without any real difficulties. Just crossed over into Iowa from Nebraska. Across the Wide Missouri.

Local authorities have shown no extraordinary interest in our grand chariot. We stopped long enough in Buffalo, Wyoming, to get the challenge sign painted out. At Mount Rushmore other tourists were friendly, so Katherine and George even invited some aboard to show off our swivel recliners and all.

The group seems to me to be more open and relaxed, more comfortable with each other, than I would have imagined possible. Some days, you'd think we'd known each other forever.

I'll tell you one thing that's different from Snug Harbor days: The diet talk has quieted down.

Back there, maybe because we had so little in common to talk about, all of us carried on about what we could and couldn't eat. Like a bunch of spoiled kids complaining about having to eat carrots or not liking squash. We discussed cholesterol and salt-free and saturated fats and fiber as if we had no other interests in the world. Every new issue of any magazine, any "breakthrough" reported on TV, was grist for our mill. Every dish on the menu in the Captain's Mess had a little heart or star beside it signifying how healthy we were destined to be. I hesitated to ask guests for dinner because I might serve the wrong food and they'd all decide I was out to clog their arteries.

Now we eat just as wisely as we all should; even on the road we have stuck to sensible food. But we have stopped talking about it. We sit down at two tables or three booths in some place for lunch and choose without dissertations about all that stuff we all knew anyway. Pleasant mealtimes. No advice floating about. Nobody saying, "Oh, I really shouldn't . . ."

All in all, we're getting along and enjoying our escape.

Except Emmett. For a while there, at Old Faithful, for example, I thought Emmett had joined the team. He smiled some, even played some dominoes and cribbage on board. But the last two days —

We angled northwest to southeast across Nebraska yesterday, Rapid City to Omaha. Out of the mountains and the Black Hills and across the prairies. The open fields and grasslands seem endless along there. Ruth and I were sitting at one of the back tables. She was working on our finances, keeping the records in order. I was messing around with this machine, tinkering with some other pieces besides this journal, for a change.

"I can't help admiring our forefathers, Ruth," I told her. We try not to speak too loudly in the afternoon. Somebody usually naps in one of the big chairs. The driver — Bess, this time — often has nice music playing. "Just look at this endless land. Spacious skies and amber waves of grain, my foot. If my husband had brought me out here a hundred years ago in some dusty wagon train and told me we'd find a promised land, I never would have gotten beyond St. Louis. Having babies in sod houses! No ties with the family and the life we'd left behind! Even the astronauts keep in touch! But those folks — I would have made a lousy pioneer."

Ruth looked around, to see if Emmett was listening, I guess. Then she closed the ledger in front of her with one big sigh.

"That's what Emmett's family did. His great grandfather came out here to Iowa from the east in the early 'eighties. As a small boy he walked behind a flock of sheep for what must have been weeks, or maybe months. It's an old family tradition that no Coleman eats lamb or mutton because Great Grandpa could never stand the smell. The entire family settled just north of Des Moines on homesteads. The place where we lived and Emmett farmed was the original family place. The Colemans had their own little world out there, one farmhouse to the next, Coleman School, Coleman Cemetery, all that; but eventually the youngsters moved into their own lives off the farms and the Coleman population dwindled. We were sort of the last of the tribe, so

Emmett's mother lived with us all those years. Then she died, and we had no children, and the farm was just too much for Emmett since help is so hard to hire unless you've got one of those great big operations."

Ruth just sat there, staring out the window.

Emmett had heard. He came to the table, pulled out the chair across from me. "No use getting all worked up about going through here, Ruth. We don't belong in this country any more. This place might as well be on Mars, for all I care. Look at all that land, all those fences to mend, all those fields to plant and care for, all that thankless work, which can be wiped out by one hailstorm or one depression. Just stop jawin' about Iowa, Ruth. We got nothin' here any more. And nobody."

Bess had us tooling along I-80 in grand style. How pleased you must be, Bess, I thought, to know what you have added to the lives of the rest of us by having the determination — no earth-shaking, world-saving affair, but making a difference in the lives of others makes a big difference to women like Bess. She turned to call to Ruth.

"Ruth, come up here, will you, and tell me if I'm right about this. From what you've told me, it looks on the map like we can turn north on I-35 a ways before we go east again on I-80 and be very close to where you and Emmett —"

Emmett was on his feet, stomping toward the front of the bus. "Oh, no you don't, Missie! Don't you even think about going up near our old home place! I never want to see that land again! We don't belong there. There's nothing there for Ruth and me any more, and there sure as hell isn't anything there we want to show to the rest of you folks. That place doesn't belong to any Coleman any more and no Coleman belongs within a thousand miles of the place. You stay right here on this Interstate. No matter what Ruth might have told you. No matter what my sentimental foolish wife might have told you behind my back, we are *not* going near that place! I never, ever, want to see that barn or that house or that stinking feedyard or that combine or that tractor or that silo!"

Remember I told you Emmett turns sort of purple sometimes? That was nothing compared to his color now. Eggplant.

I felt so sorry for Ruth. He didn't have to call her foolish. She still sat at the table, head in her hands. Everyone else was quiet, but Emmett couldn't let go.

"Why should I want to see any of the farmers around here? They haven't bothered to come to see me in California! They watch you struggling with the crops to make ends meet. They talk behind your back while you're working your butt off to hang onto your farm. They cluck like a bunch of old hens when the time comes you have to sell out. They swarm to your sale like a flock of vultures and pay next to nothing for the equipment you've invested your life in. They try to act sorry about moving off a farm, out of a house, that's been your family home for four generations. Then they all bring their tuna casseroles and their three-bean salad and wish you a joyous new life in some God-forsaken hole in the desert where you're supposed to be happy doing nothing and you never hear from them again except a Christmas card and a wedding invitation so you can send an expensive present to some kid you haven't seen in six years!

"All I want to see of Iowa is the Mississippi River! Keep driving, Ferguson. Straight ahead!"

Just when Emmett seemed to have run out of steam, one of those little red Toyotas passed us, swerving a bit. Brakes squealed. Howard Lanning half-rose from his solitaire layout to peer at the offending car. "That guy better slow down," he said angrily. The rest of us watched with him.

The red car was soon right in front of us, first in the right lane, then on the line, then it appeared to be headed straight for the shoulder. Bess hit the brakes. Hard. To our horror, that car, now just ahead to the right of us, seemed to spin back toward the roadway, and it rolled. Dust and noise and the screeching brakes of other cars surrounded us.

Bess pulled us onto the shoulder as quickly as she could, but we were a city block away by the time she got us stopped and opened the door. The red car was on its roof. Tires still spinning. Steam coming out of the radiator. Glass breaking and kids screaming. Emmett was first on the ground. He had been standing at Bess's shoulder when this began.

George patted Bess on the arm. "Good going, Bess. Just like I would have done it."

One by one we all descended, all fearful of what we might face in the wreckage of that car. Emmett, hearing the children, I suppose, broke into a run. Wentworth was right behind him.

Emmett bent over to look into the eyes of the terrified young woman at the wheel, all upside down.

"My baby!" She was trying to move. "Where's my baby? What happened to my kids? Oh, what have I done?"

Emmett pulled at the car door and Jim went to the other side. Through a broken back window, Jim pulled two preschoolers. A baby's car seat was next to the mother. Upside down. Ruth and George managed to wrench open the front door on the passenger side and fish out a wide-eyed infant. I ran as fast as I could with Bess back to the bus for some of our sweaters and blankets and such. Other cars had stopped along the way. Horns were honking. People were staring. All hell breaks loose at a time like this, I decided.

Emmett had a terrible time getting the door open on the driver's side. "We'll get you out, young lady. Turn off your ignition. Don't want a fire. Now, this door is jammed. We've got your children here. They seem to be all right. You just unbuckle that belt and let me get 'hold of your arm. I think we can get you through this window.

The girl stared. "Oh yes, sir. Oh, yes, sir." Then she gave a startled sort of gasp.

"Mr. Coleman! Why, Mr. Coleman!"

Emmett froze, then took another look. He reached in for the girl's arm just as Ruth stepped to his side.

"Here, Ruth," Emmett said, almost in a daze. "You watch to see she doesn't get cut on this glass. I'll get her out." When he had the young woman halfway out of the car, he shook his head and smiled. Smiled! "You're the Bengston girl, aren't you? I'd know that red hair anywhere!"

"Can you stand up, dear?" Ruth steadied the weeping girl as she searched for her children. Lorraine had the baby in her arms and came around to the mother. The two tots with Wentworth raced to grab their mother by the knees. "Momma," the little boy said, looking up at her, "were you scared?"

"Oh, my God, was I scared, Chris! Are you all right? Do you two hurt anyplace? Is anybody bleeding?" She kissed the baby. "Oh, thank God you were here, Mr. Coleman. And Mrs. Coleman." She stopped short, staring again. "But what are you doing here? I thought you moved to California. I thought you —"

Emmett put a big hand on her shaking shoulder. "Now I *know* you're one of the Bengstons. Annette? Marjorie? Christie? Let's see what we can do here. First, we'll try to get your things out of this car. It won't be taking you anyplace for quite a while. Get the keys, Schroeder, so we can get the trunk open. Bess, you check over these youngsters to make sure there's no bones broken. Lillian, you'd better wrap this baby in one of those sweaters in case he gets chilled. Lanning, get a wrap for our little mother here — Julie. You're the youngest, Julie, right? Now we'll have to wait right here 'til the patrol gets here. They'll need a statement. You might get a ticket, young lady. That was pretty stupid driving we saw. "

Lanning stalked over through the crowd of onlookers around the smashed car. "What the hell did you think you were doing, young lady? You could have caused a pile-up here that would have killed people! It's a wonder our driver could stop in time to miss smashing right into you. You're lucky our bus was there so you didn't have every other car on the road crashing, too!"

What the hell was the big idea? "Oh, Howard, you know she didn't do it on purpose." Lorraine took his arm.

"It was still a damn dumb thing."

The tearful redhead might have been in shock. She looked pale and exhausted to me. "Let's take the children to the bus," Bess told me, so we started off with the kids.

"I'm sorry, mister. I was just trying to get home to my folks. The kids were having a fight in the back seat and I turned around to tell them to stop it. I shouldn't have done that, I know, but I was so tired. I didn't sleep at all last night. I couldn't — I didn't —" She burst into tears.

"Oh, Mr. Coleman, I'm so glad you're here! What am I going to tell the cops? What am I gonna' tell my folks?" She sobbed again.

"I just had to come home. I had to get the kids out of there — get away from Jack — so I just loaded up what I could and . . .

"I should have known something was wrong all these months when he was so crabby and didn't come home 'til so late and all that. I should have gotten out, maybe, but I just couldn't. Then last night he came home and told me all about this other woman and all that and poor Chris tried to hug him and Jack pushed him away and almost kicked him. Started to kick Chris! And Chris is only two years old. He loves his daddy.

"So I drove most of the night while the kids were asleep and now I'm almost home and the first thing my dad will say is, 'I told you that guy was no damn good.' Then he'll give me the devil for wrecking the car."

Emmett, looking closer to helpless than I have ever seen him, put his arms around this girl, looked straight up at heaven, and guided her to the bus. "Home to the Bengstons," he said.

Those Bengstons turned out to be really nice people. The sight of our coach coming up their lane had to startle them a bit, and they were more than grateful about our giving Julie and her precious children the ride over to their farm. All in all, Emmett Coleman had handled the entire situation in stride, even Lanning's rude criticism of the poor distraught girl.

I hate to sound like an out-and-out Calvinist, but it did seem Fate had taken a hand in this affair. Ruth hugged her old neighbors with a joy I had never seen in her. Bess glowed in Ruth's happiness, really. It didn't take long for word to spread about the Colemans and their help for Julie. And their garish bus.

Before long a crowd had gathered, old friends all shrieking and kissing and carrying on. Almost every woman squealed the same greeting:

"We thought you folks had forgotten all about us back here in Iowa!"

In the midst of all this commotion, I looked around for Emmett. Where was he? Pouting behind the barn? Hunkering alone in the old outhouse? Oh, no! I found Emmett leaning casually against the tailgate of a pickup. He was telling a dozen awe-struck Iowa farmers about "carrots as big as your arm, and tomatoes ripe all year 'round. 'Course, we have dates on the trees — and all the fresh oranges and lemons you'd ever want. Ruth makes date cookies almost every day out there!"

Emmett drove as we headed on out for Chicago.

This has been another busy day.

-&

WHOSE KIND OF TOWN . . . ?

D idn't the highway patrolmen even ask about our grandiose team transportation here?" Howard sounded disappointed.

"Nope." Emmett grinned. "They were much too busy directing traffic and getting Julie's story straight to worry about a bunch of old geezers in a circus-type bus. Oh, we got the usual remarks about grandmothers, but nothing we haven't heard before. I keep hoping somebody will mistake us for the Grateful Dead. I guess we look more grateful to be alive."

I decided to commence this journal entry with dialogue. Two reasons: might make more interesting reading, and our conversation has taken a distinct turn for the better now that Emmett no longer wallows in the martyrdom of being the Iowa Outcast. Strange how many older folks think having had a couple more birthdays puts them out to pasture where the grass definitely isn't greener. Emmett had been nursing a grudge about leaving the farm ever since they hit Snug Harbor, Ruth tells me.

I mentioned that to Jim Wentworth. He has some pretty snappy replies, and makes sense most of the time. I really — well anyway, Jim got to talking about resentments that eat away at us, especially when we get to this age. He claims hanging on to resentment about someone you don't like is giving that person permission to live rent-free in your head. He's right.

Bess and I were talking about our Mr. Wentworth the other day. He was driving and we were back at the domino table. To be honest, I had been admiring the shape of his head and the way he keeps his shoulders so straight. Not a slouchy old man, this. He seems kind, too; he's always helping the "little girls" (Katherine and Sister Anne) with the slightest bags or bundles.

"I hate to say it, Lillian," Bess had a real frown going, "But every time I think he's actually come around, become part of the crowd, something else comes up that sets him apart again. Like the day he hid on the bus at Reno. How about that?"

"Well, maybe he —"

George had picked up the microphone. "Folks, Bess and I had a top-level conference this morning and came to a decision we'd like to present to you." George had on his Iowa State sweatshirt this time. Big cyclone on the front.

"Chicago should be an interesting city to visit. We have planned to spend all day tomorrow here, but Bess and I feel that wheeling this big coach around trying to see the sights of this great city would be unwieldy. We therefore suggest" — George cleared his throat — "we hereby suggest we stay in a motel outside the city and arrange to take a Gray Line tour into town."

Jim Wentworth spun around in the driver's seat. "How far out of town?" You know Emmett turns purple. Now James Madden Wentworth had taken on the color of raw swordfish.

Bess spoke right up. "We thought about Downers Grove. There are several nice motels there along Ogden Avenue."

"Fine. That's fine." No disagreement. But Jim beckoned to George after the "vote" had been taken. "Don't count me in for a room tonight, George. I have an appointment in the city. I'll meet you all back out at Downers Grove tomorrow about dinnertime. We'll spend two nights in the area?"

"That's the plan."

Funny. Just as soon as we stopped in the front drive, Jim snatched up his overnight case and a briefcase and rushed over to a cab. He didn't even wave good-bye. Just took off. There goes Mr. Mystery again, Lillian. I watched him go, wondering why I cared. Wondering if this all-important date involved some gorgeous young woman. Wondering if he would come back tomorrow at all.

Bess returned from the registration desk, handing out room keys. George prepared to park the bus. I just stood there. "Lillian, whatever are you doing?" Bess asked. I guess I surprised her by not jumping right into the routine like I always do. "Oh, just wondering," I said, feeling very dumb.

We did enjoy our tour of Chicago. Architecturally, Chicago leads the pack with Louis Sullivan buildings and other such classics. Our guide provided enough details without boring us beyond caring. We lunched in the Art Institute. I loved that part. Howard seemed to be dragging along a bit and was quieter than usual, but by now most of us were playing our basic roles, which we found very comfortable.

"One of these days we should have a display of souvenirs and postcards," Ruth said when we had all picked over the supply in the shop at the Art Institute. Katherine had a poster under her arm. I had a couple of books. Lorraine studied the museum jewelry case and wound up with some dangling earrings, which she put on at once. Howard grunted but for once said nothing. Ruth had bought a video. "We can all enjoy it some evening when we get home," she remarked.

Bess nudged me. "Did you hear that? Ruth called Snug Harbor 'home.' That's a comfortable feeling, isn't it?"

I nodded. It was a lot more comfortable than speculating about what Mister James M. Wentworth might be doing right now. Also more comfortable than wondering if he'd show up . . .

On the drive back to the motel, Lorraine spotted a sign pointing to the Morton Arboretum. "Wow! Look at that sign! Morton Arboretum! I haven't been there since I was a little girl. Went with my grandad. He claimed it was the finest in the world with all different flowers and trees, but I just thought it made a good place to play hide and seek with my cousins. Everyone yelled at us, but we'd just hide and giggle. You know how kids are."

She sat quite still. "I hate these regular tour-bus seats now, don't you? We really are spoiled with our chariot." Lorraine was really wound up. "Tomorrow could we just see the Arboretum before we drive on to — where? I'd love that."

"Lorraine, you have not asked one single thing along the way. Of course we will have time for the Arboretum."

❧

What had begun as a walk in the woods turned into another one of those days, folks. I've put aside some other writing to get this into the journal before I forget or lose even one detail. We've been to the Arboretum and a couple of other places, but I'll start at the beginning.

Emmett and George were just loading the last of our stuff into the bus when a man wearing a bright yellow polo shirt appeared. He seemed to have materialized out of a parked car as if by magic. He came huffing and puffing across the lot.

"Hey, there! You folks headed for Lakeside?" He studied the "record" on the side of our gorgeous bus. "You've never competed at Lakeside?"

"We've never even *seen* Lakeside," I whispered to Ruth.

Howard stepped up to straighten out this stranger. "Sir, we are a Florida team. Our competition has been around the country and we are most proud of our record. We do not take on all comers, however. Would you care to tell us what you consider so special about this Lakeside you speak of?"

The man could have been a second-semester sophomore showing a freshman the way to the men's room in the ad building. "Just the home of the Summer Nationals, that's all Lakeside is! You have the Winter Nationals at Fort Lauderdale." We blushed. All of us.

"Up in Ohio we have the Summer Nationals at Lakeside. Been there for years. Little early yet, but I figured you might be headed there to spend a few weeks getting used to the Lakeside courts. Competition gets pretty steep there. Pays to be ready."

"Of course," said Howard, our fearless leader with the red face. "We wouldn't miss Lakeside on a bet."

Our informant turned to walk away. The back of his yellow shirt read "LAKESIDE SHUFFLEBOARD," featuring a drawing of the end of a shuffleboard court with seven disks, three red, four black.

Much to my relief (*why?*) Wentworth was waiting for us at the motel. He seemed entirely relaxed and at ease, almost playful, which set me wondering again. Whoa, Lil!

Next morning, warm and springlike, the Arboretum filled the bill. Just the right place for a long walk. Trees budded, bulbs almost poked from the ground as we strolled by. Lorraine would have had the time of her life if Howard hadn't been along. He acted like a goon. "Well, Lorraine, did your old grandpa ever try to hide from you kids in here? Did the old man get so sick of you he suggested you all hide and he'd be 'it'? This sure bowls me over, Lorraine, all these trees with signs on 'em. Real treat, Lorraine."

I walked along with Katherine, trying to ignore this tiresome harrangue. The others stayed behind, out of range of Howard's sarcasm. Katherine pointed. "Look, Mr. Lanning, gingko trees. You don't see many of those around. Oldest tree in the world, I've heard."

"Fascinating, dear Kate. Absolutely fascinating. Do they have trees as special as that in Charleston? Oh, I guess you wouldn't know. Your old man never talked about the trees, either, I bet. Maybe Charleston has secret trees and secret houses. Nothing better than a bunch of trees on a good warm day to get you off high center. Stimulating, huh, Lorraine? Your idea, huh, Lorraine? Had enough, have you, Lorraine? Ready to get back to the orange juice, Lorraine? Carry my jacket, Lorraine. I'm sweatin' like a pig. Boy, do I love walkin' around in the woods. Should have brought some of your tasty crackers, Lorraine — we could have played Hansel and Gretel. You and Grandpa ever play that one, Lorraine? Or was your old lady always the wicked witch ready to gobble up small children and unsuspecting sons-in-law? Want to go around agin', Lorraine? We're gettin' close to the gate . . ."

I just wanted to strangle him.

I waited by the gate for the others to catch up, but Howard and Lorraine climbed on the bus right away. As Emmett and Sister walked past me, Emmett was saying, "You have a good many of these trees in your yard up there in Redlands, Sister. All we need to do is trim 'em up and you'll have an arboretum all your own."

Sister Anne's sweet smile could have melted an iceberg. "Oh, the convent is not 'my yard,' Mr. Coleman. It belongs to our Lord, you know. But I am certain He would appreciate your help in keeping the bushes trimmed."

I could have hugged them both.

Jim still had driving duty left. Before he started the motor, he turned to Howard Lanning, who had slumped in the armchair just behind the driver's seat. Howard never sat in that chair. He sat where he could shuffle. Almost noon. Jim picked up the microphone. "On to Indianapolis, folks. Bright sunny day for a nice short ride. Let's all get comfortable. Less than 200 miles. Good to get back east where the distances seem more manageable, isn't it? Commander Bess, you let me know where the lunch stop will be. Off and running!"

Why did he have to sound so pleased with himself?

Ogden Avenue at noon reminds anyone trying to get anywhere of some bad dream. Narrow and congested. Left turn lanes had been left out. Traffic tied up at every corner. "Good Lord," Wentworth said, "We'll get off this stupid road as quickly as we can." All of us watched intently as cars swarmed around us. Some of the other drivers yelled obscenities about having such a big bus on such a narrow street.

We didn't even notice Howard stumbling toward the lavatory door. He jerked it open and seemed to fall inside. We heard him bumping around in there and then the unmistakable sounds of some-one very sick. Even in the din of that mess of traffic, the sound of Howard vomiting went right through me.

Lorraine rushed to the door. Pounding on it, she started yelling, "Howard! Howard, are you all right?" How could she ask that?

Bess had moved to the back of the bus, standing beside Lorraine. Jim slowed, carefully maneuvering his way through the traffic to get to someplace to pull off. After endless minutes, the vomiting stopped — more bumping around and strange noises as Howard finally managed to unlock the door. His face ashen, he fell from the tiny lavatory, landing on the floor with his arm across his chest.

"I — I'll be all right," he gasped. "Must have choked. Can't get my breath in that stinkin' little — feels like somethin's squeezin' my chest. Hurts — like hell —" He looked up at the rest of us. "Oh, my God," he croaked. "*Oh, my God!*"

"Take it easy, Lanning." Emmett and George lifted Howard into the nearest chair. "Just take it easy. You're gonna be all right." Lorraine just stood there, staring, holding her glass of juice. Wentworth had stopped at the edge of a parking lot. He opened the door and ran toward a drug store. Bess took charge. Bless Bess. She knelt beside Howard in the chair.

"Howard, are you having a heart attack?" Lorraine seemed to have floated off somewhere.

"Howard." Bess spoke quietly, her fingers on Lanning's wrist. "I don't know, Lorraine. I'm not a doctor. I'd say it could be. Could be."

Howard sort of jerked. "God, how I hurt! This pain is terrible, terrible! I can't . . . I can't . . ." Then Howard was very quiet. We all stood thunderstruck.

"Lorraine." Bess looked over her shoulder. Lorraine had crumpled on the couch, whimpering. "Lorraine, you'll have to pay attention to me." All she did was raise her head, blank stare.

"Lorraine, has Howard been taking any medicine — heart medicine? Does he have any nitroglycerine? Has he had any attacks like this before? Lorraine, help me here! Does your husband have any little white pills that he puts under his tongue?"

"Oh, dear, no. He hasn't had anything like this. The doctor told him he ought to lose some weight — oh, Howard!" Lorraine had started to cry. "Why didn't you pay attention to the doctor? Just ten pounds, he said. Oh, Howard!"

Howard opened his eyes. "At a time like this you've gotta nag about the goddam diet! For God's sake, who's gonna help me here? Are you old fogies planning to let me die right here?" This outburst had sapped his remaining strength. Howard fell sideways, out again.

Jim came running back and started the motor without a word. Back on the street, he said, very quietly, "The pharmacist tells me the closest, best place to take him is the Hinsdale Sanitarium. It's just up the road here. I asked him to call for a police escort so we should have some help soon getting through this traffic. The cops won't have any trouble finding us, will they?"

He glanced in the rear view mirror, "How is he, Bess? Anything more any of us should be doing?"

"He's in pain, that's for sure, and he needs attention as soon as we can manage. Thank you, Jim. That was a very smart move on your part."

Sirens again, but a welcome sound this time. The patrol car fell in ahead of us and we were on our way. Howard opened his eyes momentarily, moaned, and seemed to pass out again. "Hospital? Near? Oh, God, do I need a doctor . . ."

"We're getting there now, Howard," Ruth leaned over, trying to reassure him. "The hospital is just ahead. We can see it now. A police car is leading us."

"Police? Our bus . . ."

"We can't worry about that now, Lanning." Emmett spoke up this time. "We'll get some help for you right away."

Lorraine — well, about half of this seemed to be registering with Lorraine. Sister Anne sat beside her on the couch. Silently, Sister had reached for her rosary, but Lorraine didn't seem to notice. The rest of us noticed, you can bet on that. Howard's ashen color had paled even more. He seemed almost transparent. I'd never seen anyone get so sick so fast.

The red brick building ahead resembled an old jail more than an old hospital. The police caried us into a narrow alley-like place around to the emergency entrance. Obviously, the cop had called ahead. Attendants were waiting at the door. Jim opened the bus and two young men in white coats rushed aboard. Howard tried to straighten up, to move a little.

"Just take it easy, there, old man. We're here to help." They fussed around with pulse and chest sounds and all that.

Lorraine jumped out of her chair. "Well, take him into the hospital! Why don't you take him into your hospital? Can't you see how sick he is? What do you think you can do for him out here? He needs to be in the hospital!" Her voice had reached a pitch audible mostly to dogs. "Are you going to let him die right here on this — on our — bus? I told him to go on a diet. Now here we are millions of miles from home and he has to go and —"

"Easy, lady. We know what we're doing. Your husband is gonna get the best care possible. Right now." One of the young men even patted Lorraine's hand. Others brought the cart on board and lifted Howard as if he were made of Dresden china. Carefully they maneuvered to get him down on the ground. Bess took Lorraine by the hand.

"We're going to have to go in, too, Lorraine. The nurses will need information from you about Howard and his medical history and insurance and all that. Come along."

"Insurance? Insurance? How would I know about that? Howard takes care of all that. I don't know what . . . He has some cards in his wallet. Where is he? Where did they take him? I'll have to find his wallet. Oh, damn, what a mess. I don't know about —"

Just inside the doors of the emergency room, Howard lay on the cart, obviously calmed by the assurance of medical attention. "He wouldn't let us take him on in until he talked to you, ma'am," one of the boys said to Bess.

"Me?" Bess said, startled. "You must mean Mrs. Lanning, his wife. He must want to talk to her. She needs to know about —"

Howard beckoned to Bess. By now we were all on the driveway, watching the whole procedure. "Ferguson," Howard gasped, "Ferguson, those boys in San Francisco. I'm sorry I . . . They needed help. I didn't — I'm sorry I was such a bastard about it . . ."

Bess did not reply except to take his hand for a minute. Even out where we were, we could see Howard had tears in his eyes. So did we.

"Not two hours ago I was ready to strangle that man," I remarked to Jim as we headed back aboard the bus.

"So was I, Lillian." He squeezed my arm. Seven of us waited in the bus where the policeman told us to park, waiting for Bess and Lorraine to do whatever had to be done. It must be difficult to be dealing with such complex arrangements far from home. I just hoped Lorraine was not a problem. If she started that stupid tantrum screaming again, we'd never get — never get where? Indianapolis suddenly seemed a lot more than 200 miles away.

George and Jim had had a conversation with the cop. While we sat there feeling helpless, Ruth told me the police demanded a report from our men about the incident. Names, numbers, all that.

"They even had to show him those faked-up papers from my brother-in-law Jake. I didn't dare to hang around and listen because the offer might have been suspicious. Finally, he laughed and shook hands with the men, so it must have been all right. I kept wondering if the policeman would ask what all these Californians were doing with a Florida bus and team, but Wentworth seemed to field his questions smoothly."

Ruth paused, thoughtful. "I think our Mr. Wentworth has more answers than we have questions any day of the week."

I shrugged. What could I say, after all? What did I know?

Bess and Lorraine reappeared in an hour or so. George and Bess held a summit meeting on the steps of the coach.

"How about our staying one more night at that motel in Downers Grove, folks?" George asked after due deliberation. "We ought to stick around to make sure Howard is out of the woods, and Lorraine will need to make some plans. Any objections?"

I expected him to continue like *Robert's Rules of Order.* "Hearing none . . ." But George just smiled, turned the bus around, and headed back the way we came, only more slowly this time. As we passed the police station across the street, two cops waved.

Jim Wentworth came over to the table where I was sitting.

"Lillian, it's been quite a day, hasn't it? Did you enjoy the tour of Chicago yesterday? I assume you'd been here before. Came here for medical meetings with your husband, or something? Nice town." He paused, but I didn't say anything.

"My kind of town, Chicago is." Then he laughed and so did I.

"That might make a good line for a song, Jim."

He grinned. "Let's take it down the hall to Charlie and see if he can vamp a few bars. Seriously, could we have dinner together tonight, Lillian? Just the two of us? I spotted a decent-looking Italian place not far from the motel. If it's okay with you. I'd like some time to talk."

Why had I never noticed before how blue his eyes were?

"Certainly, Jim. Fine. About seven?"

"A little earlier if you don't mind. It could be a long evening." Now what could he mean by that?

❧

We had settled into our chairs, ordered a drink (my seltzer, his beer) and my dinner companion wasted no time getting to the subject at hand.

"Lillian, thanks. I need to talk to you about two people, Lorraine

Lanning and me. Oh, not in the same breath. I just thought I ought to get to the point — or points. You are obviously a woman who wastes little time in small talk. As a matter of strict fact, you are obviously a woman of great interest and good sense as well as being good company and, well . . . let's say I want to know you a lot better for several reasons, not the least of which is your laugh. I love your laugh."

I smiled. What else?

"Let me tell you about Lorraine Lanning first. You and I — all of us — have recognized by now that Lorraine has a real drinking problem. She has the classic symptoms of alcoholism. Not only does she think she's drinking in secret, she has demonstrated great sudden changes of personality — funny one minute, raving mad the next. Sometimes she makes no sense, often because she cannot remember from one day to the next. We all know alcoholism is a disease that responds to treatment under the right circumstances. I am convinced some higher power brought Howard and his heart attack together right here on this day in this place for Lorraine's benefit. Sounds goofy, doesn't it?"

I nodded. "But I do understand what you are saying about Lorraine. She needs medical attention just as much as Howard does. So perhaps you're right about the time and place."

"My reason for such a strong feeling might sound strange, but I just learned today, in town, that Hinsdale San has one of the finest recovery programs for substance abuse in the country. Would it make sense to you that Lorraine should stay here while Howard is hospitalized — check into the detox unit and get herself some help?"

"Naturally. That does seem almost predestined. Amazing. But how does one go about convincing anyone . . . ? I've had friends and relatives who . . . Matter of fact, so many of the members of my own family have booze problems, I quit drinking at all years ago. I was on the way to the bottom myself until my sons straightened me out. But that was family help. So what can we do with Lorraine?"

"We need to talk with her tonight. But I am not about to go to her room alone. She will have been hitting it pretty hard by now, and I don't want to cause any trouble. Maybe we can both get her to pay attention. How does that sound to you?"

"Fine, Jim. Bess will back us up in the morning, I'm certain, but I'll be most happy to do whatever I can. Basically, she's a nice enough woman and we absolutely cannot leave her hanging around here while Howard is in the hospital. She couldn't cope, I'm afraid."

The waiter had been hovering for half an hour. We ordered supper

quickly because Jim appeared to have more to talk about than Lorraine
and her orange juice.

"Now. Subject number two. Me. I've been watching you, appre-
ciating you, Lillian, for a long time. But my life has been really screwed
up for a while. I straightened out most of that yesterday in Chicago and
I want to get better acquainted — be your friend — so the first thing I
must do is explain a little. No, explain a lot. But it will come in bits and
pieces. Okay?"

"Whatever you say, Jim."

"I have not been living at Snug Harbor by choice. You must have
figured that out. I honestly have not acted or felt as if I belong there. I
have been a 'guest' of the Skipper because I have been under surveil-
lance, so to speak.

"Lillian, I have tried many occupations and pastimes in my life
since I left Yale. Some have been successful and honorable. Some have
not. I have drifted, I guess, never finding the one real purpose in life
that most of the rest of you seem to take for granted. I've gone for
everything from acting to stage production to writing to gambling to
out-and-out extortion.

"Oh, I just went in for extortion once, about ten years ago, and I got
caught. Guess that wasn't my field, either. I served six years of a ten-
year sentence. My partner in crime (that's not funny) should have
gotten out when I did, but he has a rotten temper and couldn't make it
on good behavior. He was released just last week.

"My jailbird buddy and the Skipper are brothers."

I choked on my ravioli.

"Before the law caught up with us, we had stashed a lot of money
in savings accounts all over Chicago. A bit at a time. False names and
IDs — all those tricks people like me have learned from cronies. The
money belonged to a drunken old woman we found in a bar out in
Gary. We promised to invest it. We just didn't tell her we'd do it for
ourselves, not her. I still can't believe how much she trusted a couple
of bums like us.

"You're thinking about how I came up with all those ideas for the
bus, aren't you?" I nodded.

"Anyway, when I got out of jail before his dumb brother did,
Skipper decided I had to be in his protective custody so I couldn't get
all the money from the savings accounts. He sent some goons to
convince me to stay at Snug Harbor for three years. I call them the
Bright Brothers.

"Skipper has had me in an apartment, rent-free, when he could have made more than his brother and I stole — even including the interest in ten years — by selling that space. But no. Smart. Keeping me under his nose.

"Can you imagine how I felt when I knew Bus was getting out and you all had ideas about a bus trip to Chicago so I could get here without interference from the Skipper? Even the guy's nickname is 'Bus.' What could be more perfect? Unless he had been named 'Coach.'"

I snickered. "That's quite a story, Jim. So now you have it all settled?"

"Now I have served my time. I have retrieved and split the money with Bus. I went by myself over to the neighborhood where we had pulled this stupid scam and found that the old lady had been written up in all the papers for having been robbed and people sent her more money than she had ever had in her life. She celebrated by sobering up at the Hinsdale San. That's how I heard about the program there. She died and left over a million to the hospital. The papers quoted her bequest — said she never would have sobered up if she hadn't been drunk enough to get robbed."

"So that's why you left the motel in such a rush the other night."

Jim nodded. "I had to get to Bus in that fleabag hotel before he called the Skipper."

"You looked so intent upon getting away, I was wondering if you'd ever come back. I thought you might just leave us all right there without a word. But you're too nice a man to do that." I sighed, I guess. "At least, I kept telling myself you'd show up, but . . ."

"That thought had crossed my mind, Lillian, 'way back in Palm Springs when the talk first started about this jaunt — made to order for what I needed to do." He sipped his Budweiser and put the glass down thoughtfully.

"But we hadn't gotten any further than that first meeting at Bess's when it dawned on me: You were the first people I had known in my whole life who had taken me at face value. Not once has anyone of the bingo crowd asked intrusive questions about my past. Not once have I felt I had anything to prove. From the beginning, you have been willing to have me around without setting any qualifications or any limits.

"Then, when this adventure shaped up, I realized what real friends can be. Bus was amazed when I told him I was going back to Snug Harbor. But that's just what I intend to do, at least for a while."

He touched my hand. I couldn't believe it! He touched me!

"And, Lillian, Lillian, the biggest reason I want to go back there is to be near you. You are a very special person."

"Jim, you're special, too, or I wouldn't have worried about how you were spending that time in Chicago. You have no idea how many ideas I had about what you might be doing." If I didn't blush, I should have. "But now you have the money split and we can be on our way, right?"

"Right. Now I've got the money, not nearly a million, and I'm thinking about what you and Ruth were talking about. Some sort of a rescue mission at the Sister's place for kids like we saw in San Francisco.

"Have I told you enough for one night?"

He paid the dinner check and we headed off to confront Lorraine. I felt better, more in tune with the rapture of being alive, than I had felt in years. Bless Bess.

↬

HOME OF THE SUMMER NATIONALS

L orraine Lanning beamed when she opened the door to see Jim Wentworth standing there. But her smile faded some when she realized he was not alone. She patted her hair like she always does and stepped to one side.

"Oh. Won't you come in? I was just getting comfortable. It's been such a day..." She steadied herself, leaning against a chair, and started poking her foot into the shoes kicked off there.

"I feel like such a mess. And poor Howard over there in that place. And the bus in all that traffic. And the men asking all those questions. And the way Howard turned that funny color. I never saw Howard look like that before. And those people about the insurance. What could I know about all that? And the needles, all those needles and questions and tests and — but you didn't see all that, did you? Where were you? In the bus? Can I get you a drink? I'm afraid all I have is vodka. The tab broke off the orange juice can. But I could get you some 7-Up or something down the hall if you need a mixer. There's plenty of ice still floating around in that cooler."

Through all this Jim and I just stood there. Finally he closed the door and stepped toward Lorraine. "We are fine, thank you. We don't need a drink. Mrs. Morrison and I have come to find out how Howard is doing and how you are surviving after such a traumatic day. We'd like to be of help if we can."

He looked at me. Sort of a ball's-in-your-court look.

"Please sit down, Lorraine, and don't worry about the shoes, for heaven's sake. We know you've had a trying day. We just came by to be of some help, if we can." I sat on the end of the bed. Jim pulled the chair from the desk. We reminded me of two Mormon missionaries, or maybe a couple of salesmen for cemetery lots.

Lorraine sat, studying her half glass of vodka. She sniffled a little and I realized her eyes were redder than just bloodshot.

"I really don't know what you can do to help. But it's nice of you to offer. Something like this would have to happen when we're off on a trip in a strange city with a bunch of people we don't even know, actually. I kept telling Howard he should pay attention to that doctor and now here we're stuck with him in that barn of a hospital. I guess I can't just leave him there."

She held onto that glass as if it were her only friend in the world, sipped a little, then drank most of the vodka in a couple of gulps.

Jim leaned forward and tapped her on the knee.

"Lorraine, we all have a lot to be grateful for here." She stared at him, pulling her rumpled cotton skirt over her knees and patting her frizzy hair. Jim went right on, "Think how terrible it could have been for you two and for the rest of us if Howard had gotten this sick out there on one of those long stretches of road without a town or a hospital or a doctor within a hundred miles or more. That traffic was bad today, but endless miles of prairie with a man close to dying would have been worse."

She nodded, not taking her eyes off the glass in her hands.

"Lorraine, my husband was a surgeon," I said. "For years we had heard about the Hinsdale Sanitarium because it's one of the best hospitals in the country. The staff here has a fine reputation. Howard will have the best of care here, you can be certain of that. Like Jim says, we could have been out in the hinterland with no care at all."

"Yeah," she muttered, "or we could have been back home in Jeff City where we had our own doctor and I could sleep in my own bed with my own things and my old friends and my own kid around to take care of ... everything. Now here I am with you people and I don't know what to do." She emptied the glass in one swig and stared at it, surprised. "Excuse me. I need another drink."

James Madden Wentworth stood to his full six foot-plus and took the glass from her hand. "No, Lorraine. You do not need another drink. As a matter of fact, Lillian and I came here to talk to you about that very problem. And about what could be a most fortunate circumstance in your life."

Lorraine laughed — a throaty, vulgar laugh. "Fortunate? In my life? Me? You don't know me very well, mister. You don't know what you're talking about. Oh, I might look fine to the rest of you old goats, but how would you like to be married to somebody who makes fun of you all the time? Some boring old toad who does nothing but play solitaire all day long? Some leftover bootlegger who never got along with his son or paid attention to what you wanted out of life? How would you like that? Huh? I need a drink, I said. Or are you deaf in your old age?"

Jim did not lose his composure or his smile. "Do you think for one minute that we have not all been aware of your drinking problem? This trip has only confirmed what we have observed at bingo and on other occasions around Snug Harbor. You're not fooling anyone, Lorraine, unless it's yourself. We came in to talk to you about treatment for you. Here and now. Howard will be well taken care of. No doubt about that. You need help just as much as he does. You're just as sick as your husband, lady. You might as well face up to it. Now." He sat down again.

I moved a little closer so I could touch her hand. "Lorraine, if we were not fond of you and Howard — we do consider you to be our friends — Jim and I would not be here. You have shown all of the classic symptoms of alcoholism, my dear." Damn. Why did I say it that way? I hate myself when I'm so condescending. My dear, my foot.

At any rate, I tried to make the point. She was pulling away, hunching down into the chair.

"Alcoholism honestly is a disease, Lorraine. You display the symptoms by your frequent lapses of memory. How often have you forgotten who won at bingo or when it was your turn to hostess our Wednesday coffees? You also drink in secret — at least you convince yourself it's a secret. We all saw the bottles of vodka stashed under the bar on the bus or even in the overhead compartments behind your makeup case. We understand when your personality can change mid-sentence from amiable to outright bitch. We've seen you skip meals and carry that orange juice around like some sort of sacramental wine. Alcoholism is not a disgrace, Lorraine, it's a disease, and it can be treated and controlled. And Hinsdale San has a program renowned for its effectiveness. And here we are."

"So what makes you so smart, Mrs. Doctor's Wife? How dare you talk to me like this?"

"Alcoholism affects almost every family I know of, Lorraine. I've learned from experience."

"How or why we both know what we're talking about is beside the point." Jim was on his feet again. "You've heard all this before, haven't you, Lorraine?"

"Oh sure. There's always some fuddy-duddy who doesn't want

anybody to have a good time so they start telling you about how you drink too much. Sure, I've heard it. Back home I heard it from my sisters and my kid. He nagged me all the time about his dad and me and how he decided we were drunks. Why do you think we moved away? And why don't you preach at me about Howard? He drinks, too, you know. He can't yell at me to quit because he knows he'd have to quit, too. And I don't drink all the time. He drinks even more than I do. When I know he's gonna start in on me about the bills or about the way I do his shirts, I just . . ."

"We know what you 'just,' Lorraine." I knew she wasn't going to say anything else. She'd talk a lot more but she wouldn't say anything different. Just over and over the same stuff. I've known a lot of drinkers. "Now, let's talk about some help for you out of this mess you're making of your life before it gets any worse. Let's talk about getting you well, not just Howard."

"Here? Now? Well, I suppose I could talk to somebody when I go back to see about Howard in the morning." Lorraine had her eyes on the cooler near the desk. "Maybe there'd be some sort of therapy . . ." Long pause. "As long as I'm stuck here until I can move Howard back to —"

"That's not good enough, Lorraine. Lillian and I have watched your behavior for three years now. We know what kind of a drunk you are. We know and you know that if you are left here in Chicago with your husband in the hospital you will get yourself in all sorts of trouble. You'll go into your cute little stewardess act or have a tantrum about the service in some restaurant or find some traveling salesman around this hotel to tell your troubles to. You know that. Deep down, you know that, don't you, Lorraine?

"You've been drinking heavily now. You need help now. We are the only help you have here and we intend to do whatever we can. Now. Not tomorrow. Not back in California. Now. Forget about that bottle in the cooler or the one you must have hidden in your overnight bag." Lorraine jumped. "You need help and you are going to get it. Now."

Why hadn't we talked these details over before we came in here? I tried to get a clue for my next lines from Wentworth. Lorraine seemed to be listening, in spite of all the vodka.

"Jim's right, Lorraine. Now is the time. Any time you waste, like waiting until morning, will only be a step backward. I suggest I can help you put together whatever you will need for a hospital stay, Jim can call the hospital about our arrival and get a cab, and we'll get out of here.

You won't need much. Ruth and I will bring the rest of whatever clothes you want in the morning. Then we can take most of your luggage right along on the bus. Okay, Lorraine? Okay, Jim?"

The rest of the night went pretty well. Actually, I'm too tired to write much more about it. Lorraine did throw one fit when we headed for the cab. Claimed everyone in the motel was watching us take her prisoner. After we arrived she gave the attendants a hard time and refused to answer some of the questions, but that's par for the course. We can let the pros handle that. At least we are leaving both of the Lannings here in good hands. Bess has called to tell their son about the entire course of events. We didn't even know they had a son until now.

❧

Day number 11 for the Golden Roamers — minus two. Now only eight of us are on the bus (I've given up calling it a coach — sounds too much like Cinderella, and this is no longer a fairy tale), but that's fine. We miss the sound of incessant shuffling of cards, but the doctors tell us Howard and Lorraine should both be in shape to rejoin us in Phoenix in about two weeks. All we can do is keep on rollin'. After all, we haven't seen the dogwood in Pennsylvania or the old houses in Charleston, yet.

This morning Bess came up with another of her fine ideas. Bless Bess. She brought the road maps to the breakfast table and pointed out the one spot which had had all of us wondering.

"I have located Lakeside," Bess announced, with not a little excitement in her voice.

"Right here," she pointed. "Not far from Sandusky, Ohio. On Lake Erie. Here. Lakeside was one of the original Chautauqua institutions. I found some, not a lot, about it in the Triple-A book. They say it's a church-related resort with sports, lectures and concerts but it's not really open until next month — third Sunday in June. The Triple-A does not mention shuffleboard, but I was thinking, since we're headed in that general direction, we might find out . . ."

"Good idea, Bess." I, your faithful journal-keeper, cannot say who said that first. I think we all did.

"In that case, we stay right here on I-80 and 90, cross Indiana, and head for shuffle-land. Off we're gonna shuffle even on to Buffalo, since the Mother House is in upstate New York."

We stopped for lunch in Toledo, feeling strange about our reduced number. In the—what, ten?—days since we pulled out of Snug Harbor we have gotten used to being with each other. Now we can sit at one long table at Denny's or Shoney's for lunch instead of needing to split up. Not traumatic, but I do hope we don't lose any more. Wouldn't feel right in such a big bus. Especially using so much gas.

After lunch we chose to stay with the state highway, No. 2, to get to Lakeside. Actually, Lake Erie has a nice shoreline and the drive was most pleasant. Emmett had the map in his lap and the microphone at the ready so he could point out the best parts. Crane Creek State Park looked like a fine bird sanctuary, although Emmett couldn't say just what it was.

After Port Clinton we headed out to the tip of a peninsula toward Lakeside, Put-In Bay, and the Perry Victory and International Peace Monument. Emmett really shone on this one. He had the Triple-A book open to the right pages and made certain we were fully informed about how Admiral Perry in the War of 1812 defeated the British in the Battle of Lake Erie. Perry had a terrible time because the British were much better equipped than were the fledgling American forces.

Somehow, it astonished me to think of our early history taking place in Ohio. I think of Ticonderoga or Bunker Hill or Charleston, even, but not Ohio. That shows you how much I still have to learn.

Lakeside sits on the tip of a peninsula. Nearest town appears to be Marblehead. Across Lake Erie toward Sandusky we could see the ferris wheel and roller coaster of Cedar Point Amusement Park, but Lakeside clearly has its own charm. One of the signs proclaimed Lakeside has been here since 1874, founded as a Methodist conference ground. And this is the Mecca of shuffleboarding? My skepticism was getting the best of me as we drove through the stone pillars onto the grounds.

Victorian houses lined the streets and we spotted several little parks. The business district of the settlement stretched no more than three blocks beside a large auditorium and the clubhouse of the Women's Club. Bed-and-breakfast signs hung on porches along the tree-lined streets. Basically, anyone could see the relationship of Lakeside to Chautauqua, but the New York location seems, well, better kept.

The pavilion on the lakefront overlooked nice beaches, however, and the long pier seemed inviting even on a not-so-very-warm day for May. Trees and paths and benches and screened porches told us why Lakeside has survived. It's a comfortable, relaxing place. Quiet, particularly off-season.

On the lake shore we parked beside a big old frame hotel and decided to explore what we could. I wouldn't say the place was deserted. An occasional pickup truck and a workman or two seemed to be the entire population, but we walked across a nice park toward a miniature golf course and a dandy bandshell before we heard someone yelling. A woman was coming at us from one of the houses facing the park, and she was in a hurry.

"This old gal means business," Emmett commented. "Hope she's not runnin' us off for walkin' on her grass."

"Hey, you shufflers! You there, you shufflers! Welcome to Lakeside! 'Course you're a month early, but shufflers are always welcome here. I'm Mary Montague. I belong to the Shuffleboard Club here. Live here year 'round. I heard your bus driving in —" she looked around at the hotel parking lot — "dear heaven, what a bus *that* is! You must be some shuffleboard team!"

Bess extended her hand. "Well, we try. Of course, we are not the whole team. Others will be joining us along the way. We're just touring, playing when we can, and getting acquainted with other . . . other shufflers along the way. We've heard about Lakeside from other —"

"Well, I'd sure expect you have heard about Lakeside. Come on over here. You might think you've seen shuffleboard courts before, but how about this? We have about fifty here. All well surfaced. All lighted. Covered bleachers, and some rain protection for the courts, too. Ever see anything like this, folks?"

We shook our heads without saying a word. There before us we beheld a layout for shuffleboard that must rival Wimbledon for tennis or St. Andrews for golf. Each court had its own scoreboard permanently mounted at one end.

"Of course, we're not all set up for the season, yet." Our guide pointed to an enormous sign above the roof sheltering the courts. "SUMMER NATIONALS," it read. "Come June we get all set for the Nationals and the preliminaries that go on here. Of course, our whole summer is busy. We have tournaments all the time with the clubs from Akron or Toledo or Columbus. Not Cleveland. No club in Cleveland. Some of our members just spend all summer vacation here. Shuffling. Whole family joins in. We just live shuffleboard around here."

Sister Anne had been right up front while Mary carried on there. "Mrs. Montague," Sister spoke so little and so softly that her voice startled me. "Mrs. Montague, at our convent in . . . the south . . . we had a shuffleboard deck, we called it, where the other sisters and I used to play this fine game. I just loved it, but I might have forgotten some of the finer points. Would it be at all possible — I mean, could we possibly — even if it is a little cool out here today — could you show us? My teammates and I are a trifle rusty from all this travel, and we're not really sharp competition."

You could have knocked us over! Certainly I had seen that faded shuffleboard at the old mansion. All grown over with weeds, as I recall. But here Sister has known all along more about this so-called game than the rest of us combined— and she was too polite to say so.

"You betcha, Sister. Come right along over here. The manager's not here yet, but I can let us in for some practice stuff. Of course, the real players bring their own sticks. Some bring three or four to have a choice depending on the drift of the court they draw for tournament play. Some old guys move in here loaded down with their own equipment like Minnesota Fats."

Mary Montague rummaged around in the shed for a minute and emerged with a cup filled with something like sand.

"Of course these courts haven't been readied for the summer, yet, but we can sprinkle these glass beads on to make a better surface before I show you how to —"

"Glass beads? You're kidding! You sprinkle glass beads on this shuffleboard place?" Emmett was paying attention now. "But this game is just a matter of —"

"A matter of skill, mister. Real skill. That's why any age can play and practice makes perfect. Some folks play here as much as eight hours every day just to get their balance and their control right. You don't need to be strong to play shuffleboard, sir, but you need to be smart. Who wants a practice session? Long as we're at it . . ."

Bess grinned. "We all would appreciate some of your expertise, Mary. Thank you. Our coach suffered a heart attack in Chicago, so we are now without top-flight guidance. Could we all have a lesson or two? Many of the players who won those titles and matches listed on our bus are no longer with us, so we need all the help we can get."

I sighed with relief that we had left the manatee T-shirts in the bus. This woman would never stand for anyone making fun of her or Lakeside or the entire sport. More than a game, obviously and very serious business.

I took the stick handed me over to one side so I could fish out my pocket notebook. Too much to learn here to risk our own memories. I needed to take notes.

First of all, the disks for real players are yellow and black. Our little-kid sets had red and black. Mary Montague dropped terms like "draw for line and partners," "hammer," and "kitchen," all of which I needed definitions for.

George and Emmett helped Ms. Montague spread the glass beads, then one or two at a time we lined up to play sample shuffleboard.

~&

I am here to tell you — whoever you are — that this game has much more to it than we had realized. Emmett had trouble because he hit the disk too hard. Mary showed us where to place each shot so that we were protecting other scores or blocking other players. Really. I tried the stance and felt awkward. My disks ran off the side or over the end. I think I'd better get my own stick, preferably a lightweight steel number with a spring built in. Those look snappiest. I'll get that when I buy my new convertible and get my hair cut short. Might as well start a new life all at once.

We had the best time, all eight of us. George got the control better than the other men but the star of our class was Sister Anne. That gal really knows her shuffleboard. Next time we get into a tight spot in a parking lot, we know who can get us out.

The euphoria came to a screeching halt when Mary dragged out the big book for registering teams at Lakeside. "Do many players come up here from Florida?" Bess asked.

"Of course," said Mary Montague. "They play the Winter Nationals down there in your home territory — you must know that — then they come up here. You probably know a lot of those players. Some real champions down there. Have you met Martha Jewett or Phil Sullivan? Both great players. And Martha's husband is even better than she is — sometimes. You know them, I'm sure. At least you've watched them play."

Bess said not a word. She handed the register to Wentworth, who scribbled something on a couple of lines and glanced at his watch. "You know, Miss Ferguson, this has been one fine experience, but we'd better load 'em up and get on down the road if we plan to keep to our travel schedule. We lost a lot of time in Chicago. Let's get going."

You never saw eight old folks move so fast! We stopped only to wave goodbye and shout thanks to Mary Montague, standing there holding four sticks in one hand, shaking her head.

"What did you write in that book?" I asked Jim as we headed out of there.

"'Thank you for a nice time.' What else could I say?"

I like his grin more every day.

⮑

SURPRISE, SURPRISE, GEORGE!

How could anyone ever ignore the beauty of upstate New York? We spent the night on the outskirts of Ashtabula, then followed I-90 around Buffalo. Remembering Ruth's words about not having seen much of the United States because of being so cooped up on the farm with her mother-in-law, I did suggest a side trip to Niagara Falls, but Bess murmered something to Ruth. Ruth nodded and smiled. Then Ruth said, "We can see that next trip, can't we? Emmett?" Emmett didn't even nod, but the matter seemed settled. I guess one of these days I'll figure out what that was all about.

At any rate, I'm here at the table where Howard usually shuffles, writing and riding in perfect comfort as we exclaim over grand old barns and the locks along the Erie Canal.

How can anyone forget the size of upstate New York, come to think about it? Crosswise, this state goes on forever. It took us most of the day to get to Utica.

Sister Anne had been studying the maps. "Oh dear," she sighed, as we all joined the map-study during lunch in a diner in Palmyra, "Going to the Mother House will take us too far off the main roads. Clear up to Schroon Lake. Perhaps I could just get a regular bus, or maybe —"

"Hitchhike, Sister? That might be a good idea, but the traffic must be pretty light up in the Adirondacks this time of year. Might be hard to catch a ride. Maybe you'd like to rent a bike? Oh, no, dear lady, the first part of our deal when you stored the bus in your barn involved your visit to the Mother House. We wouldn't miss that for the world."

Jim Wentworth traced the road to Schroon Lake with his pen. "You stay right with us. That way we all get to go. Right?"

We all nodded. "Schroon Lake?" Katherine whispered. "Whoever heard of a place called Schroon Lake? But at least we will know where it is when we get there. We won't have to hope to find the Mother House, will we?"

I have to admit the thought had crossed my mind. If Sister Anne had so little mail and no support from this nunnery, they just might have gone out of business. Visions of overgrown shrubbery and dead trees did float by.

Jim had been right about how easily we could drive to Schroon Lake. As inviting as some of those roads look in that huge green part of the map — the Adirondack Park — we had only to follow one Interstate to another to find our way easily to Schroon Lake.

We did cut cross-country from Rotterdam up to Saratoga Springs to reach I-87, the Northway. I would love to stay longer in Saratoga Springs, but we have our timetable set now. For some reason, we have an urgency to move right along.

Today is the 28th of May.

Here is my latest — and possibly my last — poem, *Song of the Open Road.*

> *Fourteen days and counting*
> *Since we left Snug Harbor's shore.*
> *Life is looking up now —*
> *More worth planning for.*
> *We've faced some minor crises;*
> *We've learned of kids and dope.*
> *More aware now of the prices*
> *People pay in search of hope.*
> *Two are left behind for treatment,*
> *Two have yet to face their tests:*
> *First the Mother House, then Charleston,*
> *As we help friends in their quests.*

I think before I let anyone see this journal, if I ever do, I'll take out all my poems.

At any rate, we are on the road now and the country is beautiful — wide expanses of wooded hills with gentle gray mountains in the distance. These Adirondack Mountains seem more feminine, more appealing, than the majestic Rockies. We saw little of Lake George from the highway, but Bess suggested driving down by the lake for lunch. Bless Bess. Another great idea.

In a quiet (off-season) village called Bolton Landing we enjoyed a friendly lunch with a view of the island-garnished lake, which absolutely defies description. The colors, the water, the stillness, and the pine-covered islands simply overwhelm my senses. The next exit is Schroon Lake.

~

Wishes do come true, even on old-people busses. Here we are back in Saratoga Springs after a mighty eventful visit to the Mother House of the Order of St. Ives. We all agreed on the need to spend one night in the village of Schroon Lake, then part of the following day. We had to give Sister Anne enough time to make her reports and explain some of her problems.

Actually, that "following day" was only this morning. We drove back down here to Saratoga Springs after some interesting talk with the Mother Superior. Tomorrow we head on down the road for George's old stomping grounds in Pennsylvania.

I put that paragraph in mostly to orient myself when I have time to read this account.

The Adirondack Lakes have inspired artists for centuries. Schroon Lake had the same magic as the rest. We drove slowly through the village and George asked directions to the Mother House at the combination filling station and general store. The convent stood out like a sore thumb on the east shore of the lake near the north end.

White frame buildings with old green roofs occupied the crest of one hill above the water like God had placed them there on the final day of creation. A road lined with cedar and pine trees wound up to encircle the main house. Cottages and a barn or shed stood guard on the outskirts. I fully expected to see Julie Andrews whirling and spinning across the horizon, singing at the top of her lungs.

Our splendid vehicle barely fit on that road. The branches scraped the sides as George carefully maneuvered up the hill. In mid-afternoon, the place appeared to be deserted — well kept, but unoccupied. On the outer rim of the circle drive, George stopped the bus. "I guess I'd better not just honk to let them know we're here. What do you suggest, Sister?"

Sister Anne managed a weak laugh. "No, Mr. Schroeder, that might not be such a good idea. Perhaps it would be best if I simply ring the bell. The doorbell."

With that, George opened the door of the bus, Sister stepped down to the gravel lane, and the front door of the Mother House opened as if responding to some spiritual command.

Two nuns, one old, one quite young, could not have been more surprised had they seen Julie Andrews there, too. The younger one ventured down the porch steps, the other just held on to the railing, peering through Coke-bottle-bottom glasses into the bright sun reflecting off our green-and-gold chariot.

"Yes?" the youngster called as she approached. "Yes? May we help you? Have you lost your way? This is a closed convent, a cloister. We do not sell Amaretto cheesecake or train dogs. You must have taken a wrong turn. You must be looking for one of those others — maybe New Skete or —"

The girl stopped in mid-sentence. Her habit, though a bit mussed, matched Sister Anne's. The same cape shoulders, the same headgear, the same everything.

"Why, Sister! Why, Sister! You're one of us! Where did you come from? How did you get up here on that —? What is that —? Oh, I must call the Mother! Right away!" And off she darted, back across the path to the porch.

By now we were all standing outside the bus. Jim put it into words: "That girl used *The Sound of Music* as a training film. She still watches it during meditation every other Thursday." I shuddered a little, but Sister Anne laughed loudest.

"You never can tell about the younger generation, Mr. Went-worth," she smiled.

Now the porch had filled with nuns. At least six of them stood in awe of our monstrous transcontinental coach looming in their meager driveway. They parted as the waters of the Red Sea as the Mother Superior emerged from the side door. This was one big woman — even outweighed me by more than a pound or two. Her veil fluttered just so in the breeze as she stomped over to where we stood. Her entourage followed obediently.

"Just what is the meaning of this? Did you not see the "PRIVATE PROPERTY" sign beside our gate? There are no sightseeing tours here and we have no public rest rooms."

Most of all, she had been glaring at the three men in our party. We might as well have been the Donner group asking for food or a load of teenagers on a scavenger hunt.

Finally her steely eyes landed on Sister Anne.

"Why, whatever —? Who —? Is that you, Sister Anne? No. Can't be!

Sister Anne? My, how you have shrunk. What are you doing with these
. . . people . . . from Florida? Have you deserted our mission? Have you
left our Holy Order? Have you decided to be a social worker after all
these years?"

"Oh, Mother Mary Lucy, didn't you get my letter? Of course I am
Sister Anne. You must remember me. We were novitiates together so
many years ago." She stopped with a grin. "We both have changed
shapes, I'd say, but it's good to see you. These kind people had some
trouble with their . . . bus . . . and I helped out a bit in California, so they
offered to bring me here on their circuit of shuffleboard tournaments."

"Well, that seems most kind, but we do not welcome strangers
here. Our work is —"

Lillian, I thought, you have been the ride-along, take-it-as-it-
comes laptop-pounder of this group until now. High time you get this
straightened out before Sister Anne gets her feelings hurt and we leave
here without accomplishing a damn thing. That's what I said to myself.
After all, I am the one who stood ready to direct traffic while my girl
friends fixed the bicycle. I have a vested interest here. So I stood right
up to confront this Hitler-in-drag before matters got any worse. Toe to
toe. Eyeball to eyeball.

"Mother Superior," I tried to be as tall as she is. "Our driving in here
today is no act of tourism. Sister Anne is our friend. She did not bring
us to the Mother House just for a view of the lake and a tour of these
lovely grounds. She has told us many times of the beauty of this place,
however, and she did not exaggerate the wonder of it. Nobody could.
But we have come off our intended path today only because Sister
Anne needs and deserves help."

The mother squared her shoulders so I took a deep breath. Okay,
girlie, here goes. Both barrels.

"Your mission at Redlands certainly doesn't look like this. Have
you seen it lately? Have you been aware that this dear lady keeps that
mission going by sheer will power? She has barely enough money to
keep herself and her cats fed. She serves and comforts the poor and the
needy to the best of her ability, but getting around that town full of hills
on that awkward bike would challenge a woman half your age. Or my
age. Or Sister's age.

"The shrubbery is overgrown. Only two rooms of that monstrous
house are usable, the sun room — the chapel — and the pantry. You
cannot even see the shuffleboard court there. Sister keeps the altar in
perfect shape with the help of the Altar Guild from St. Leander's on the

Mexican side of town. They give her their old linens and their candle stubs, which they probably got second-hand in the first place from some wealthier church downtown. Except for a crippled old man who shows up to fix the chain on her bike, this tiny woman bears the entire burden of your mission and she needs to be recognized by the rest of you people here."

I stopped long enough to let her reply, which she did not.

"Now Sister — Mother — Reverend Mother — some of us have a plan to discuss with you which could be of great service to your flock and to your order. But I must say we have been mystified by the lack of support, financial and otherwise, from this end of the St. Ives network."

"Mystified? Surely you must be aware that the Queen of Missions in Redlands was fully endowed by the generous benefactor, Mr. Burrage, from its establishment in 1930. Mr. Burrage's sister, our Mother Superior Helen Cleone — God rest her soul — assured us of the continuing financial support from annuities or some such included in this wonderfully generous gift in honor of their mother. We here have known of Sister Anne being somewhat on her own there, but how can you possibly be out of money, Sister? What have you done with all that? How many cats do you feed?"

Sister Anne never lost that smile. "Oh, dear Reverend Mother, the financial support established in 1930 has never changed. I know nothing of annuities or trust funds. I just know that Mr. Burrage left a continuing fund of seventy-five dollars a month sixty years ago and it has never changed. I am certain the entire convent could get along well on seventy-five dollars every month in those days, but that barely pays the light bill now.

"I have contacted the Bishop, as you know, but he insists we are not under his jurisdiction. All alone, I can scarcely put on a bazaar or run bingo games to raise money. Other parishes besides St. Leander's help a little, once in a while, but since we do not really belong in the diocese . . ."

"Come on in, Anne. We need to have a talk." The chief nun halted on the path, looking over her shoulder at the rest of us. "We do have a receiving room here inside. The other sisters will be happy to bring you some tea. Do come in."

On the wall of the reception room hung pictures of the Queen of Missions in Redlands in all of her glory in 1930. The contrast with the weed-engulfed stucco-shedding place we know was an astonishment.

"Now that's where I used to play movie star," Bess remarked when she saw the pictures.

"It must be lovely there," one of the sisters sighed. "I wish I'd been sent there, but we need so many of us here and so many of the younger ones —"

"What about so many of the younger ones, Missy?" Emmett was really interested. "Why aren't there more of you folks out there to keep that place going?"

"Well, sir, I guess you'd say more of our sisters find their calling to do the Lord's work among the poor, the needy, of the cities. Seven of our number now live and work on the lower east side and in the South Bronx. California being the land of plenty and all, we felt the needs were greater among the urban poor, the homeless."

"California the land of plenty? My foot!" Emmett had his dander up now. "Don't you ladies know there are homeless, helpless people out there, too?` You New Yorkers seem to think you have a corner on everything including poverty. Not so, lady. Have you read Sister Anne's reports she sends all the time?" Emmett stopped short. He turned around to face the other nuns in the room. "Has *anybody* read Sister Anne's reports?"

"The dispatches from the Queen of Missions were always kept for Mother Helen Cleone until her death. Now I really can't say where..." The Sister who said this must have been about forty-five. She had a very red face, at least at this moment.

Emmett was about to continue this harangue, but Sister Anne and the Mother Superior had joined us. We all shut up.

"So," said Mother Mary Lucy in a much softer voice than we had heard before, "Just what might be this plan of yours?"

Bess, as usual, had the nod from all of us to be the spokesperson. "Reverend Mother, you might have heard from Sister Anne about the young man we managed to help by chance during our short stay in San Francisco." She nodded.

"You might also have surmised the nature of this group. We are basically retired people who find ourselves with time and energy on our hands, but not much to make our days worth while. We are, in short, sick of these golden years of leisure. We want and need to be of some use and some service just as much as the homeless or hungry might need our help.

"Putting those two factors together in the Queen of Missions — an ideal spot now serving less than its maximum potential — should turn out to be a good way to carry on your original intent but in today's world."

"That sounds fine. Very noble. But funding for such projects comes with difficulty. We live a life of poverty here and get by. What you suggest —"

"What we suggest we have adequate funding for, at least for a decent start and establishment in the community." Jim had stepped forward, facing the boss as I had done earlier. Only he was already taller. "Just as Mr. Burrage's generosity gave you the mission, just as an anonymous benefactor has supplied this bus to make this trip, so an even more anonymous donor has supplied the funds for this mission to the needy, the out-of-step, the addicted, and the generally distraught people of the Redlands-San Bernardino area. All we need is your permission, Madam."

"You have my permission, sir." retorted Mother Mary Lucy. "But you'll need more than that. We here in New York should reset our goals to participate more in this work in the West." She spoke as though it would be necessary to hire scouts to lead her nuns to the workplace.

"Manpower — womanpower, actually — will be crucial. This we can literally work out overnight, with your permission. Would you consider leaving Sister Anne here with us to iron out details? Perhaps you all would enjoy the short drive to Fort Ticonderoga in the morning. then return about noon for a simple luncheon with us here. By that time, Sister will be ready to get back on the road, I'm certain."

"That works for me, Reverend Mother. How about the rest of you?" Bess wheeled around to all of us. We headed for the door. As a matter of fact, we were all ready to get back on our bus, and Fort Ticonderoga sounded just fine.

Just as we started boarding, the Mother Superior shouted from the porch. "By the way, would there be room for two or three more on that wagon? Sister Anne will need some help when you guys get your whirlwind going!"

❧

So that took care of that. I was so proud of Jim about the money. For a man who has led the pillar-to-post existence he claims, he has real polish. But he did mention Yale, didn't he? At any rate, we are paying more attention to each other since our dinner together in Chicago.

But now I'll close this machine for a while. Jim and I plan a walking tour of Saratoga Springs before dark. I hope the race track isn't too far. Oldest in the country. Just right in this Victorian town.

Tomorrow we'll smell the chocolate at Hershey, see George's old home town of Annville, Pennsylvania, on Memorial Day, and begin to get acquainted with two new passengers, both nuns.

❧

Bess has some sort of a secret. I think she has told part of whatever it is to Ruth, but they are saying nothing to the rest of us. The reason I say "part of it" is because I noticed Ruth apparently asking some question and Bess saying, "You'll find out. Just be patient." Wrong time of year for Christmas, but Bess gives me the feeling a surprise is not far off.

The drive to Annville, Pennsylvania, from Saratoga Springs was a doozy. The longest stretch we've had so far. Usually we take it easy — leave about nine in the morning, stop in time for dinner. Not today. We were on the road before daybreak, heading a long way south and west through Binghamton, where Bess allowed us minimal breakfast before we lit out down across Pennsylvania like we had a tail on fire.

Thank goodness I-81 has been widened all the way. Bess drove first, then turned the wheel over to Jim with almost a command — "We're not wasting time today, Jim. Move us on out!" Not that we were taking unnecessary chances, and we all had this sense of urgency, but only Bess knew why. And maybe Ruth, but she wasn't telling.

Shortly after noon we reached the big intersection at Indiantown Gap Military Reservation. I-81 and I-78 come together there. Bess picked up the microphone. "We are approaching Pennsylvania Dutch country. Will you pull into the next rest area, Mr. Wentworth, to turn command of this craft over to Captain Schroeder? We will now head toward Lebanon, Pennsylvania, where we shall turn south or west or whatever on 422 in order to arrive in Annville."

The two new nuns were delighted. This adventure had come upon them so suddenly it had taken most of the morning for Sister Anne and Katherine Haley to fill them in on our routines, our itinerary, and the identity of each one of us.

These girls, in their early thirties, I'd say, were particularly interested in the San Francisco adventure and how we plan to operate a rescue-rehab in California. They also asked many astute questions about the visit to Lakeside and the shuffleboard instruction.

"Of course, we play all summer. It's good exercise for us at the lake. But we really don't play by the rules, I guess," Sister Frances Jo Ann admitted.

Sister Helen Eugene agreed. "We get into some real squabbles at the convent because nobody really knows the rules."

Katherine held out a small yellow book. "Read this when you have time. That's the rule book Mary gave me at Lakeside. Looks complicated to me, but you youngsters can figure it out."

George sat so square in that driver's seat tooling down that narrow road to Lebanon, he might have exploded if we had spoken to him. I started to ask about the hex signs on the barns, or about what crops had been planted in the fields, but I could not bring myself to interrupt his concentration.

"I never knew these bridges were so narrow," he said, mostly to himself. Or maybe he was talking to Esther. Sometimes he does that. Sometimes, when he's driving, he talks to the bus, like he was soothing a skittish horse or encouraging a worn-out old nag.

"I don't smell any chocolate yet," Ruth called from her seat in the back.

"Just you wait 'til we're past Annville, Ruth. That's when you smell Hershey. Just you wait."

"Does Hershey come before or after Annville?" Ruth asked.

"After. So don't hold your breath. It might be a while." Once more Bess gave us that mysterious tone.

"These new nuns will think they're stuck with a bunch of nuts," I said to Jim.

"Do you think they aren't ?"

"Well, we haven't always been so . . . I don't know. I feel expectant, but I don't know what to expect."

Right then we passed the sign saying "ANNVILLE."

"Show us that park right by the church, George, will you please?" The request came from Bess. "I'd like to see that town memorial."

George turned the corner of the narrow old street — to be greeted by a blast of trumpets that could have been heard all the way to Harrisburg. Suddenly a swarm of people shouting and waving "WECOME HOME" banners surrounded the bus.

George looked as if he might faint. He stopped the bus and just sat there. He didn't say anything. Didn't move. Just sat.

"George," Bess said as gently as she could, "These old friends and neighbors of yours are having their Memorial Day picnic. They want you to join them. Don't you think it would be polite to get out of the coach and say hello to these folks? They've been waiting for you. This is why we hurried so today. You are the guest of honor at the picnic!"

What a secret that turned out to be! Bess had been arranging this. That's why we couldn't waste time at Niagara Falls. We had to be here in time for George to make a speech.

Men, women and children had gathered at the door of the Golden Roamers chariot. They began pounding on the side of the bus. The trumpets started up again.

Finally, George moved. He opened the passenger door and motioned the rest of us to get off first. Then, with all of the townfolk and all of the Roamers gathered 'round, George Schroeder stood at the top of the steps, took one deep breath that sounded more like a sob, and got down out of the bus.

That little man was a study. I thought of him on that first day of this adventure when we asked for the hundredth time if he wanted a ride and he refused. I could picture him out on that busy freeway, waving his arms to attract our attention in all that traffic. And I thought of him saying, "Esther would be so proud," when he first maneuvered this monster into that little shed. Now here he stood facing at least half the population of Annville and maybe more from surrounding towns, all welcoming their favorite faithful bus driver for a holiday picnic.

One woman shoved past me — must have trained with the Steelers. She threw her arms around George's neck and squealed like a teenager.

"Oh, George! Georgie! I thought you'd never get back here! Even when your last letter said you might have a surprise for me, I didn't dream you'd be showing up right here in town driving this enormous bus! Oh Georgie! This is the best surprise I ever saw on Memorial Day! Even better than the air circus that time! Better than we ever had here, I'll tell you!"

George managed to disengage this creature. I've told you that Emmett has been the color of eggplant and Jim's complexion has resembled raw swordfish, but George had them beat. George was the same shade as a fresh-cut flank steak. He turned to those of us standing closest.

"Friends, I'd like you to meet Esther's cousin, Gladys. Gladys Scheideman. These are some of my friends I met in California — but they're from Florida. Yeah, these are my Florida friends I met in California, and this is Esther's cousin Gladys."

You should have seen Bess. I won't say what color she was.

"How about this, Bess?" I asked her. We stepped to the back of the crowd as George moved toward the park, being clapped on the back, shaken by the hand, and just generally bounced around in high spirits.

"How about this is right!" Bess replied. "Here I break my neck to get ahold of the city fathers here to tell them their homesick boy is coming for the Memorial Day celebration hoping to chase away his blues about his dead wife and his neglectful son. I make Ruth swear within an inch of her life she wouldn't tell the plans to have George drive in with bands playing and Lebanon bologna and German potato salad coming out our ears, and he's already made a date with his wife's cousin! 'Oh Georgie!' Did you hear that? He's been writing to her all along! And we thought he was so pathetic! Not only did he find a bus to steal, he found a way to haul his girl friend back to California with us!"

Bess sat down on a bench, absolutely beat.

Then she started laughing. Bess laughed so hard I thought she might choke. She bent over double in near-convulsions. Jim and Ruth came over to stand with me and stare at her. Finally, she held up one hand and tried to get her breath.

"Don't you see?" She waved over toward the center of the crowd, where George was laughing and talking and greeting all comers, meanwhile trying to disentangle himself from the clutches of Gladys Scheideman.

"Don't you see? George has had this long-distance romance going on, and it's fine. It's time he found someone else. But he's been too shy to tell any of us about it. He had plans of sliding in here unnoticed and bringing Gladys away on our bus before the town got wise. He wanted to be the knight in shining armor slipping in to rescue the fair maiden before all the other old witches in town could talk about him and Gladys. And Esther.

"So I spoiled it all by thinking I'd do him a big favor with a celebration of his homecoming, arranged with the committee. Now old George has to make a speech and he can hardly talk!"

"Maybe he can hardly talk, Bess, but you sure have jazzed up the day for the rest of this crowd. Look at them." Jim nodded toward the locals. Standing around in bunches, heads shaking, tongues wagging, teeth clacking and gossip spinning, all of Annville had the greatest excitement since Gettysburg, no doubt about that.

"Well, let's go try some of that famous Lebanon bologna so we won't have to eat again along the road. They might have some shoo-fly pie, too."

I just wanted to smooth it over some way.

Bess snorted. "It won't be as good as Esther's. I will never understand men or marriage."

I'm not sure why, but Jim winked at me. Then he squeezed my hand.

Oh, wow! As the kids say.

THE HALEYS, THE GRAFTONS, AND THE MIDDLETONS

Well, dear reader, whoever you are, we had to catch our breath after those last two stops. Seeing the Mother House and explaining Sister Anne's predicament had been a trial for all of us, but picking up the two younger nuns to go along made the entire effort worth while. They certainly are nice girls — girls in their thirties, I'd judge.

Sister Helen Eugene stands at least a head taller than our little old friend. Her warm smile has to reflect an inner glow. She borders on radiant most of the time.

When the Mother Superior asked Helen Eugene to accompany us and to help with the plans for a renewal of the mission's mission (I could not say that any other way), we were delighted. She had impressed all of us in the first five minutes with her warmth and enthusiasm, which seems to grow almost hourly. She and Emmett have already made basic plans for shrubbery-trimming and location of the vegetable garden. Helen Eugene's ruddy complexion should fit right into working the grounds with Emmett. They sort of match.

The other Sister, Frances Jo Ann, is just tall enough to make stairsteps when the three of the nuns stand together. Middle kid. All three wear their habits all of the time, although the Reverend Mother did suggest they could feel free to wear other clothes for gardening in the California sun. I doubt they own any other clothes, judging from the size of the black satchels they carry. We can take care of that when the time comes.

Frances Jo Ann grins a lot. She loves to make jokes and has already asked for driving instructions. Other than that, and the fact she's most pleasant to have on board, her interest in shuffleboard seems most important. Bess has already appointed her the new coach. I guess my best word to describe Frances Jo Ann would be "wholesome." I won't say that aloud to her. I used to be called "wholesome" while I was growing up. Aunts invariably used that word instead of coming right out and saying, "my, that girl is big for her age!" I won't pull that on this blessed Sister. She's heard it before. These new passengers add immensely to our depleted number in more ways than one.

Then we have Gladys. Gladys Scheideman. Esther's cousin. I would be skirting the truth if I claimed we were all most welcoming. As Bess had said, it honestly is time for George to come out of his shell and enjoy life with someone, and if Gladys is to be that someone, so be it. I certainly haven't noticed any women around Snug Harbor who would fit with George, although most of them have tried. As soon as word got out that George had no wife, the casserole brigade formed on his doorstep.

He has stayed pretty much alone or with our group. I had once fantasized that George had met someone "off campus" since he took so many bus rides, but I guess his love affair there was with the bus. We all should be grateful for that. Without George and his dreams, we would not be here, headed south through Maryland toward the Carolinas. Believe me, George deserves our thanks and our consideration.

None of us ever knew Esther. She died before George made the big move west to be near Sonny. Matter of fact, we don't know Sonny, either. His car shows up at George's every two or three months, but he never stays long enough for us to get to know him. In spite of the shock of Gladys grabbing our little friend by the neck and practically strangling him with joy, we should give the woman the benefit of the doubt. If George wants her, she can't be all bad. Loud, boisterous, energetic, but not all bad.

And that's the way we are all reacting. It could not have taken more than two hours for Gladys to pack up whatever worldly goods she needed and come right along with us. In front of the crowd of old hens clucking at her as she prepared to join our "tour" I invited Gladys to room with me. That gave George a little breathing space and we left Annville with our respectability intact.

Gladys might look like Esther. I've been trying to remember the pictures on George's sideboard. Most of them were taken in the thirties, so Esther has always seemed to me to have had bobbed hair, and almost ankle-length housedresses with very little shape. Gladys, on the other hand, is mostly shape. Her hair might be home-permed and have more than a dash of red added. But she has a sweet face and a contagious laugh. Last night she started telling me about some of the picnics they used to have and how the boys threw the girls with their long skirts into the horse tanks. And how she and her husband had always been best friends with George and Esther, as well as relatives. So it goes.

~

We headed straight south with no more side trips.
Bypassing all of those cities didn't bother me a bit. As we drove away from Annville, all of us had a sense of urgency about getting on to Charleston, I think. Bess was driving down the freeway, humming about the Toonerville Trolley. Our on-coach routine had become quite comfortable. Yet, the closer we approached Katherine's goal of locating her husband's boyhood home, the more unease I felt among all of us.

"Strange," I remarked to Ruth sitting beside me on the couch. She had some needlework she'd picked up at the Mother House. "I have almost mixed emotions about this leg of the trip. How do you feel about it?"

"Lillian, you surprise me. It's all worked out well up to now, hasn't it? I mean, we've had a surprise or two, from Lorraine and from Jim — maybe — and certainly from those hoodlums in San Francisco, but I thought you wanted to get on down south without stopping in New York or Baltimore or Washington. We could still do that if you feel we're short-changing ourselves. Lord knows the next cop might not be as easily handled as the others have been, so maybe we should be seeing more —"

"Oh, my, no, Ruth. We all voted to head straight for South Carolina, and that's fine. What I mean is, back in Snug Harbor, Katherine carrying that picture around was almost an inside joke. We all said, 'Here comes Katherine and her picture.' Now the joke might turn into a reality that could be more than any of us have bargained for.

"Her husband practiced with another group of physicians, a rival group, to be honest, in Colorado Springs. My husband never had much to do with Haley. Thought he was some sort of a threat to his own practice, I suppose. Nobody fusses more about the competition than surgeons, or acts more sanctimonious about it to outsiders. Consequently I have no idea what sort of skeleton we might be pursuing in some Charleston closets. Neither do you. Neither does Katherine, I'm certain. Do we honestly want her to find the truth? That smug little 'banty rooster,' as John always called him, might have had some pretty sordid background to keep it hidden even from his wife and kids."

Ruth laid her embroidery on the table. "You're right, Lillian. Emmett and I talked about it last night. What do you suppose we'll find down there? Probably nothing. But I'm not sure that would be so bad, going back to California no wiser about that house and its secrets. One secret inside another." Ruth laughed. "I can see us ten years from now sitting at bingo saying, remember the you-know-what we hunted for, you-know-when?"

"Possible, Ruth. Possible."

Behind us, at one of the tables, Katherine and Sister Anne seemed to be having some sort of a planning session. Those two tiny ladies have become close friends and they are a matched pair. Could be two Hummel figurines or old-time paper dolls. I could hear them, but tried not to act too interested. It was obvious their conversation was not as negative as Ruth's and mine. Katherine had the picture out, of course. She had every detail firmly fixed.

"You see, Sister, these houses of Charleston are all long and narrow and built with a long porch along one side. They look sideways to the houses you and I are used to. I've made quite a study of the architecture since Edward died. He never would talk about any of it, of course. But this house does have a different look to the more experienced eye, I'm told. Notice this sort of Gothic arch over the entrance. And the shield or crest carved in the stone above it. Then see the corners? Those are quoin corners, larger blocks of this cut coral rock that make the corners stronger and give the house this sort of 'outlined' look. One of the historians I talked to — he made a fine speech at the art center some years ago and I sneaked down with the picture to ask questions — said the details on these Charleston houses tell family histories from Colonial days."

Sister Anne nodded happily. "It would be a lot easier, my dear, if one of these details was a number, wouldn't it?"

"Oh yes, Sister. But who are we to let a small problem like that get in our way? Now as soon as we have checked into the hotel . . ."

Interstate 95 absolutely tears through Virginia and the Carolinas. We did pay more attention, all of us, when the road signs in Virginia pointed to Manassas and Richmond, Fredericksburg and Petersburg. Familiar names to say the least. George picked up the microphone. "Now, I don't want to interrupt your dominoes, Emmett and Jim, or distract you ladies from your conversation. But it does occur to me we are passing some country very important in our history here, and I have a suggestion."

"Oh, George," Katherine called from the back of the bus, "It's fine if you all want to stop here along the way to see some of the battle-grounds and museums and all that! We don't need to be in that much of a hurry to get to Charleston on my account." From the sound of her voice, I was almost convinced she was serious.

George had raised one hand, waving her off. "No, Katherine, I don't mean let's stop now. I mean right now might be a good time for us to start thinking about our next trip. Maybe next year we'll want to —"

Everyone absolutely whooped and hollered. You should have heard them. "Ye gods, Schroeder, we aren't half-way through and you're planning for our next trip?" Emmett's laugh was louder than any I'd ever heard from him.

"Why not? A fine leisurely journey to the Civil War spots might just be the ticket. In a year or so."

For some reason, we all grinned at once, and I felt much better about the prospects at Charleston. In spite of the fact we hadn't won a game yet, we certainly were reacting like a team.

Bless Bess.

We swooped right on across North Carolina, commenting mostly on the abundance of pine trees and outlet malls. Does anyone pay retail anymore? Even the tobacco companies had outlets along here. Imagine, outlet stores for cigarettes in this day of enlightenment about smoking and all that!

Bess remarked about those signs. I moved up behind her while she was driving so we could chat a while. Actually, I haven't volunteered to drive, although almost everyone else has. I figure they enjoy it. I love my own car, but wheeling this monster down the road doesn't appeal so much. I might have to park it.

I keep my word processor set up on the smaller table in the back so I can make notes along the way. That's what I'm doing right now, as a matter of fact. Then in the evening in my motel room I can go over it all and print out the day's journal. These are mini-disks; I make one for each day and label them. In case you wonder how my writing this up is being managed, I'm pleased. This is my version of life in the fast lane.

We stopped for gas near Fayetteville and changed drivers. Jim's turn. He has been known as our "clutch driver" since the harrowing experience in that dreadful traffic getting Howard to the Hinsdale

Sanitarium. Even George had been complimentary after that. He had a hard time trusting other drivers, at first. Dear George! None of this would have happened without him.

Bess, Ruth and I sat around the game table — the larger one — after our shift at the gas stop. (That's another good thing I might not have mentioned. We all move around — fruit-basket upset — whenever we stop. That shuffles us all as much as Howard shuffled his cards.) Sister and Katherine were still deep in conversation, but now they were on the couch.

"I have a question for you two that might sound silly, but having never been married, I just can't fathom something here." Bess had lowered her voice and leaned toward us across the table. She pushed her coffee cup aside. "Can you tell me how some woman could be married to a man for forty years or so and never know precisely where he came from or anything about his family? This story of Katherine's has not made sense to me from the beginning. How can you live that close with someone and not know —?"

They both looked at me. "Well, I've wondered about that. Now mind you, I didn't know the Haleys all that well back home, but I've seen those couples from our generation. Typical of the adoring student nurse who married the older doctor and carried that hero worship through their married life. I wouldn't be surprised if Katherine referred to what's-his-name as "Doctor." Many of them did. Besides, they must have been married in the mid-thirties. Men had moved just one cut beyond considering their wives as chattel. More like wholly owned subsidiaries. That was my husband's attitude, anyway. Wives were told whatever was suitable for them to know back then. Some women accepted that role. Some of us didn't. At least, not quite so much. Doctor's wives aren't much different than anyone else, but some of them surely used to think so."

"I'm fascinated you should ask the question, Bess." Ruth had poured more coffee and pulled her chair close. Emmett was dozing in the recliner with his back to us. "I used to spend a lot of time reflecting, I guess you'd say, about being a farmer's wife. Basically, life on the farm gives a woman more independence than almost anyplace. I mean, you can plan your own day. Chores might pile up if you don't keep to some routine, but your time is your own. Except for having meals ready on time and getting up at the crack of dawn. We never had children, of course. That made one big difference.

"On some of my down days, when the crops were hailed out or

especially after we had Emmett's mother to put up with for thirty long years, I used to think about "the farmer takes a wife." I could skip all the in-between verses and go straight to "the cheese stands alone." At least, I felt that way until we got into this trip.

"But Katherine . . ." Bess smiled. "How about her? What if we find something terrible?"

"For Katherine, by this time nothing could be more terrible than not knowing," I told Bess.

Scattered palms and groves of live oaks festooned with Spanish moss could be seen along the highway as we approached Charleston. The outskirts looked almost like any other city — food chains all lined up in a row, strip malls, motels. George turned on the air conditioner.

Katherine had moved to the chair behind the driver. We were all watching her more than the scenery.

"I have something to tell you all," she said, as if addressing a multitude. Without the Lannings, there were eleven of us now. "No matter what happens here, no matter what we might learn or fail to discover — either one — I cannot tell you how much I appreciate your kindness in coming here with me. I can't say how many years it has been. Perhaps the house has been torn down. Perhaps nobody in Charleston has any interest in finding this place. Perhaps this is just a wild goose chase, like Emmett has said. Maybe it's just an old woman's dream, a fanciful . . ."

Katherine's voice broke. She started to cry. "Anyway," she sniffled, "I thank you for your indulgence." Then she stiffened a bit. "Tonight you will all be my dinner guests in the hotel."

Jim Wentworth moved to the chair across from Katherine. He had been sitting next to me. "Charleston will be a fascinating part of our trip under any circumstances, Katherine," he said softly. "Your quest has given each of us a more personal interest in the city. After all, more battles of the Revolution were fought in South Carolina than in any of the other colonies. All of us have some heritage here. And the Civil War began right in this harbor at Fort Sumpter, although I understand we should refer to that conflict as the 'recent unpleasantness' and not be shocked when we are referred to as Yankees. After all, some still call that the 'war of northern aggression,' I understand."

Katherine's reference to Emmett's "wild goose chase" remark had struck a nerve with our Iowa farmer. He stood beside Katherine's chair until Jim saw him and moved back to the couch. Then he sat, uncomfortably.

"Could I have a look at that picture, Mrs. Haley?" By now we were in the older part of town. "Seems to me a good number of these houses look like that one."

"Oh, dear, Emmett. I'm afraid they all look like this one."

"Nope. I haven't seen a one with that crest thing, but several have the heavy corners."

Heavens. Emmett had heard it all. I thought he'd been asleep. Had he heard our conversation about marriage, too? I could hear Ruth again, saying, "the cheese stands alone." Oh, well.

George pulled us up in front of the Mills Hyatt House and we attracted quite a crowd. People just stared at our bus. No different, except we had stayed in less-splendid hostelries along most of the way. This one suits our needs here because of the House Hunt. The historic district is right here, and so, we hope, is The House.

You won't believe this, but Katherine Haley leaped off that bus the minute George opened the door. She had that damnable picture in her hand and her purse flung over her shoulder. She headed straight for the doorman. "Young man, have you ever seen this house? Here in Charleston?"

"No, ma'am, I can't say I have. But you might ask our tour desk. We have all sorts of guided tours of the historic district. They might know of that house. We've got a lot of 'em here."

I watched her as we checked in. She asked everybody who walked by. One man said, "Sorry, lady. I just got here from Cleveland." I'm happy to report that almost everyone smiled, but nobody said, "Why do you want to find it?"

"You know, Lillian," she said while we waited for our keys and such — even eleven people seem to be a chore for hotels to sort out in spite of their computers — "these houses look alike 'til you study them. Some have six panes in the windows, some nine. Double windows can be six over six or nine over nine or six over nine or nine over . . ." She sounded like a domino game.

At dinner this evening she questioned the waiters and the maitre d'. She showed the picture to the girl in the newsstand. It's a wonder she didn't run up on the bandstand and ask the bass player. No luck. Not even a nibble.

I'm here writing up the notes of this arrival in Charleston, but I'll tell you a secret. Looks pretty bleak to me.

❧

Better news here, folks. I haven't had a minute all day to record much more than a few scratches on my pad, but there's more tonight. I moved the word-processor to my room, or rather Jim brought it up for me when he knew I'd want to get this down and get set for tomorrow.

I spotted Katherine out on the sidewalk talking to some black women selling baskets before I ever dressed this morning. That little figure darting around waving that picture was a sight. Maybe instead of a word-processor I should have bought a video camera. Whoa, Lillian!

Anyway, the basket-sellers were all shaking their heads. No luck again. By the time we gathered at eight for breakfast, Katherine had her day planned.

"There is only one picture here. I can show it to only one person at a time. Therefore, why don't the rest of you go on about the sightseeing here and I will meet you back here about cocktail time?"

Sister Anne sat stiff as a ramrod. "I shall stay with you, Katherine. Two heads, you know."

I had to smile at the way Jim Wentworth looked at those two tiny old women. Determination just radiated from them. Jim didn't hesitate. "I shall escort you ladies. Let's get going." And off they went.

Once or twice during the day we spotted that strange-looking threesome. Jim so tall, the women so little. We came out of the Powder Magazine and saw them getting into a cab. Then about five o'clock they turned up again, right on the corner of Church and Water Streets, where they had started in the first place. Jim looked to me like he had had it. He had that "headed for a Budweiser" aura about him. Sister had wilted a bit, too.

But as Ruth and I watched from the entrance of the hotel, Katherine stepped off the curb toward a car stopped for the light. She thrust the picture right under the nose of the woman in the car, who sort of screamed, I thought. "That picture must be dog-eared by now," Ruth said, laughing. But this was different. All of a sudden, Katherine was herding Jim and Sister Anne into the back seat of this car. The lights had changed. Horns were honking. Our friends disappeared into the traffic. So much for the beer, old buddy!

Naturally, we could hardly wait for our gathering for dinner. What on earth had happened?

Katherine told the story. Even the waiters listened and grinned.

"I just asked them again if they had seen that house. The man asked why I wanted to know. I said I had come all the way from California.

That's what did it, don't you think, Sister? The coming from California part." Katherine had to stop to catch her breath.

"The man — his name is Middleton — was the one who told us to get in. He was driving. His wife — Mrs. Middleton — was most kind. She said they could show us the house since they live not far from it, but when I told them my husband's name was Haley, they looked like it might be a mistake. I just prayed. I'll bet you did, too, didn't you, Sister?" She didn't ask Jim that question.

"Mr. Middleton said he had always known it as the Grafton house, even though he thought the name sounded familiar. He also said the house stood vacant for years and the neighborhood kids thought it was haunted, but now a young couple — He drove up past it, and it is! It absolutely is the house in the picture! No doubt at all! It's Bermuda limestone coral. That's *pre*-Revolutionary. And I met the young woman who lives there, and we're all invited for coffee in the morning!"

Finally Katherine shut up so we could order dinner. She discussed wine with the waiter.

Wineglass in hand, Katherine stood at our dinner table. "I propose a toast to you, my friends who have helped me. I wish to thank especially Mr. Wentworth and our dear Sister. Such patience and endurance you have shown!" When she sat back down beside me, she winked.

"You're right, Lillian. Jim Wentworth is a nice man."

❧

NOW WE ALL KNOW

Well, I sat up half the night at this machine, working on the journal from yesterday. That, as usual, is an exaggeration: One, I went to sleep before midnight, I'm sure. Two, writing this journal can by no stretch of the imagination be called work. I am having the time of my life. Each day, something new!

Bess rang my room shortly after dinner to report that she had had a call from the Lannings' son. Both Howard and Lorraine are well on the road to recovery and they plan to rejoin our gang in Phoenix when we get there. Good news. Bess keeps in touch with Junior and has been a real encouragement to the Lannings, I'm sure. Bless her.

Now about today. What you see here is my morning preamble. Often I find myself looking back as well as forward — back to our Snug Harbor days of planning. So far, so good, I'd say, insofar as our original purposes were concerned. We certainly have livened up all of our lives.

Sister Anne has gotten squared away about the convent. Emmett seems much more relaxed about life in general, although the old Emmett has not disappeared completely. George looks like the man who hung the moon every time we are complimented (which is daily) about our splendid conveyance. Sometimes I get the feeling that having this trip and this bus and Gladys too might be more than George can bear.

And now today. Oh, dear reader, today outshines them all!

Today we shall proceed "in a body" to The House. With any luck at all, we might learn something about the mystery that has haunted Katherine Haley's life for more than fifty years. Wish us luck!

Noon. Back at the hotel.

What a house! What a morning! What a story!

We arrived, bus and all, precisely at ten o'clock. Mr. and Mrs. Middleton were there with this dear young couple to greet us. Katherine was an absolute picture herself in a most becoming coral and turquoise print silk, matching shoes and sweater, of course. She must have been up all night doing her hair. She looked like Barbie's grandmother. A bit heavy on the rouge, but . . .

Nothing would do but that we have a complete tour of the house, and I must say it is a grand example of classic Charleston. Patty, the new owner, showed us the renovation they have already accomplished. They have a long way to go to get back to the ultimate in preservation, but I'd say this old house is in loving hands. And seeing each room gave a good background for the astonishing story Tom Middleton told us as we sat on the piazza with our coffee and pastries.

Katherine's exuberance in each room tickled me more than anything. She could not keep her mouth shut.

"Oh, look at this!"

"Oh, how lovely this is!"

It did not matter what "this" was.

"My, dear, this room has such grace!"

She complimented everything including the wastebaskets and the plumbing fixtures.

Sitting on the piazza in a very large chair, Katherine dabbed at her nose with her fanciest handkerchief, looked all the way around her, and said softly,"I have seen the Acropolis, the Eiffel Tower, and the Great Wall of China, but I never thought I'd see this house. It's more of a thrill than all the others combined."

She turned to the Middletons. "And the gardens are wonderful."

Mrs. Middleton (I never did get her first name) moved to a stool beside Katherine's chair and took her hand. Her husband stood as if to make a speech.

"Mrs. Haley," he said, "after my wife and I brought you here last night, it started me thinking. I told you I thought this place was haunted when I was a boy. We always called it the Grafton house. Now I have something here you might want to see, but I'm not sure . . ."

Mrs. M. seemed embarrassed. "He rummaged through drawers and boxes half the night looking for these clippings," she said quietly to Katherine.

Middleton picked up a large manila envelope and opened it carefully. Yellowed newspapers. Katherine gasped. "Why, that's the same picture I have!" she cried.

"Yes. That's why I picked you up on that corner. Usually we don't cotton to people hunting for old houses. They're either bargain hunters or some nut from the Preservation Trust, but you had this same picture."

"These are dated 1917. And it does say Grafton house. Whatever does —?"

Katherine carefully unfolded the fragile newpaper to see the headlines.

"Oh, my!"

Tom Middleton held the paper for all of us to see. The headline was bold and prominent:

LEADING CITIZEN SLAYS WIFE AND LOVER
IN FIT OF PASSION

"Shall I read the rest?"

"If you please, Mr. Middleton. I'm afraid I can't do that myself." Out came the hankie again.

"'Edward Hollister Grafton III has been arrested and jailed in connection with the shooting death of his wife, Mary Lucinda Haley Grafton, and an unnamed consort. The crime of passion occurred about midnight in the ancestral Grafton home on the Lower Battery. The Graftons have been leading members of society in the city. One son, Edward Haley Grafton, has not been seen since the shooting. A search is under way for the sixteen-year-old lad.'"

Katherine did not say a word.

"Mrs. Haley, any of us hates to be the bearer of bad tidings. I am sorry, but you asked. My wife and I debated about showing these to you, but I decided you ought to know. Perhaps you will understand your husband's reluctance to talk about his family.

"You see, my father, who is now in his nineties, was the best chum of your husband. I called him this morning to refresh my own memories of this gruesome tale.

"As a mere lad, Edward heard the shots in the bedroom and rushed in to find this terrible scene — his mother and a man he'd never seen dead and bloody in the bed. His father, drunk as a lord, standing in the room, waving a big old pistol in the air. Mr. Grafton kept yelling, 'I told her I would! I told her I would!' When he realized his son had come in by the other door, he leveled the gun right at him and started to cry. 'Get out of here. Get out! You're no good, either — just like that slut of a mother of yours!' At least, that's the story as Edward told it to my father that night when he hid at our house while the police were looking for him. Witness, I'd guess."

None of us spoke. What could any of us say? We were suddenly strangers again.

Middleton continued in a minute. "As soon as daylight came, Edward Haley Grafton — Dad refers to him by all three names— sneaked out of our house. He said he was headed north and nobody heard from him again except for one letter, which I could not find. I'll keep looking. The boy said he had taken his mother's maiden name and enlisted in the army — the AEF. Nobody ever heard from him again, so my father and our family assumed he must have been killed in the war. I heard the tale years later and thought the house must be haunted because such a terrible thing had happened there. As a matter of fact, my parents refused to answer questions about it for years, and it wasn't even our folks involved."

Wentworth broke the silence. "What became of the father?"

"Fine old southern family, you know, and no witnesses. He was acquitted after pleading crime of passion and temporary insanity, or some such. He became a recluse in this house and eventually drank himself to death."

In the silence, a bird fluttered in the magnolia tree. A boat whistled out in the harbor. We Golden Roamers Shuffleboard Team sat as statues in the old southern garden.

Katherine broke the quiet. "Edward carried all that grief and pain all alone all those years. I do wish he had told me. I always thought he was ashamed of me and I was not worthy to be included in his fine family. He could have explained, I think, but I'm not sure I'd have told anyone if such a thing had happened to me. I might have been afraid I'd be judged for my drunken father or my adulterous mother.

"You have been most kind to find this newspaper and to tell me this. I have always been most proud of my late husband, Mr. Middleton. He was a lot older than I, and a handsome little man. I was only a student nurse when we met, but he had a gentlemanly quality I adored. He was decorated for bravery in France and went back to serve in the Second World War, as well. I'd say he lived a successful and honorable life as a Colorado surgeon, wouldn't you, Lillian?"

Did she have to ask that?

"Certainly, Katherine. Certainly."

Obviously, our mission had been accomplished. We all stood as if on command, ready to march along. Before we had a chance to babble our thanks and say goodbye, Tom Middleton raised his voice.

"Now, Mrs. Haley, I promised my father I'd do my best to persuade you to call on him with me in the . . . home . . . where he lives now. He will be more than delighted to learn of his boyhood friend's successful life and to meet his widow. I have been prepared to ask to drive you over there to see Father, then I would deliver you to the hotel."

He stopped as if embarrassed.

"But that was before I caught sight of your glamorous transportation. Tell me — this is asking a lot, but would it be too much trouble for y'all to drive over to Royal Siesta Palms so my father could see that chariot of yours? Some of those people get pretty depressed over there, and I'm certain just the sight of your bus would . . ."

"No trouble at all, Mr. Middleton." It was George, of course. He had the driver's cap in his hand. Clapping it on his head, he squared his shoulders and looked as if he were ready to check our tickets. "Why don't you and the missus come right along? We've plenty of room. Just give me the directions. We can bring you right back here. Do you think your father or some of his friends might like a little ride, too?"

❧

Back in the saddle, only this time we have even more to congratulate ourselves about. This certainly has turned out to be a greater adventure than the Bobbsey Twins ever had on Cherry Island.

Our next scheduled stop will be Phoenix, where we will be rejoined by the Lannings. Can it have been three weeks already?

Well, not quite yet, but almost. Right now we are in pleasant country, crossing south of the territory most of us know. Of course, we steered clear of Florida. Don't dare to get too near to be too closely scrutinized by the shuffleboard buffs. But Atlanta and Birmingham made good stops for some of our needs, like a laundromat close to a park and that sort of thing.

Our added passengers are fitting in well. The three nuns haul out the shuffleboard equipment every evening and have the best time playing in some parking lot while the rest of us just hang around. Bess usually joins in for doubles. These girls know most of the rules, now, so we are well fixed for our next encounter if we run into one. Gladys spends her time hovering over George. It's nice to see a couple our age so, so fond of one another.

Now here comes my secret for the day. I think I know how Gladys feels. Remember I told you about Jim Wentworth having such a nice smile and how I have admired his kindness to some of the others? Remember I told you he squeezed my hand that time? Remember how I reported watching him with the sister and Katherine in Charleston? Remember how uneasy (jealous?) I was when he raced off to Chicago? Remember how you used to feel in seventh grade when you "liked" a boy?

In spite of the fact that I have been positive such a thing could never happen again in my life, I am truly more than interested in James Madden Wentworth. Probably I am blushing as I write this. After all, how many years has it been since I . . .? Well, you know. But here I sit, almost frothing at the mouth telling secrets because somewhere inside me this girl still lives. Someplace deep in there I have been aware of the same stirrings that made younger years so exciting and me so vulnerable.

Not since the days of our high-school "Sub Deb Club" have I so wanted to tell another girl how he looks at me, how he almost kissed me when we walked back to the motel together after dinner last night. I know, I just know, he's feeling as I am. But here we are surrounded by all these nuns and everybody and I have Gladys in with me and he rooms with George.

Do you hear what I'm saying? Do you believe it?

Whenever we get on the bus I try to sit close to him without looking too stupidly obvious. I'm sure he does the same and sometimes I think the rest of the crowd must be chuckling behind our backs, but I might never know. At least we will be back at Snug Harbor in just a few days, now. I can hardly wait.

Do you know how long it has been since I wished someone would kiss me ? Or hold me close ? Or feel warm and comfortable beside me?

What sort of talk can this be for a woman pushing seventy?

☙

PURD GETS THE MESSAGE

Y>ou can be either the statue or the bird. That's right. On any given day, the choice is up to you. My dad always told me that. "You can either be the statue or the bird." And if you have more than three "statue" days in a row, you are in bad trouble.

This greatest of truisms has been ricocheting in my brain for the past week — thinking mostly how proud old Dad would be that I haven't had a "statue" day for almost a month now. Neither have any of the other Golden Roamers, who used to specialize in statue days back at our old home place, Snug Harbor.

As a matter of fact, when we stopped in El Paso for lunch and laundry, I ducked into a near-by hairdresser's and had all my hair cut off. Just a mite longer than a crew cut. Forty years with a knot on the back of my head is enough. Now I'm sorry I hadn't been shorn long ago. Easier, quicker, and (Jim says) quite becoming. The rest of the crowd have complimented me, too.

Ruth and I have collected some interesting clothes along the way. Sportier, you might say. We don't look like Golden Roamers who used to specialize in statue days back at our old home place, Snug Harbor.

We've had a good time here in Phoenix. Everyone breathed a sigh of relief when Howard and Lorraine appeared right on time to meet us at the hotel. Howard has lost some weight and his color is good. Lorraine certainly doesn't have her Mexican-jumping-bean syndrome working like she used to. She's quite serene. I hope it lasts. At least until we get back home.

Now, that brings up a change I want to discuss with you. When we all felt trapped in our cubbyholes at Snug Harbor, weary of the same routine and not really acquainted with our neighbors, "home" meant back where we came from. For several days now, one or the other of us on the bus has referred to "home" and meant Snug Harbor. Remarkable! We are actually looking forward to getting back — when our biggest reason for risking this stolen-bus caper was to get away!

Enough of the preamble for today.

By the end of this driving day we might be turning in to the drive at the Queen of Missions on Sunset Drive in Redlands. First, we are going to play one real shuffleboard tournament. Howard figured out from the newspaper that we can enter the Sun City Open tournament. One morning, no more. Well, we've come all this way, dragging our equipment, and we haven't much to show for our hours of practice, so why not?

My motto from now on: Why not?

After noon we can take off for California. Bess explained it to Sister Anne and Katherine.

"We haven't done much night driving, but now it makes sense. We can all get our cars from your barn and drive home without being noticed, and Jake can take the bus to his shop before daylight. Okay?"

Katherine glanced at Sister Anne and smiled. "Why not?"

Her motto from now on: Why not?

❧

The shuffleboard tournament was great fun. I think when we get home to Snug Harbor I'll get a stick of my own and start playing.

The crowd around the shuffleboard courts in Sun City made me gasp. I hadn't seen that many people since my last Kentucky Derby, I guess. All sorts of team insignias around, and plenty of official-looking men and women wearing badges. Howard stepped up to the registration tables and put our names in. Just the three nuns, Bess, and the Colemans entered.

First of all they had to draw for partners, which shook the nuns a bit. Mixed doubles had not been on the agenda up at Schroon Lake. The Sisters fit right in, however.

Ruth's name had been drawn by a scrawny little man wearing a Sun City T-shirt and pink shorts. "Do you play by Lakeside rules?" Ruth asked, as politely as she could ask any question of an eighty-year-old man in pink shorts.

"Wha'd ya' say?" the old man shouted.

"Lakeside rules! Do you play Lakeside rules?"

"Sissie, I just send 'em on down the line and knock you plum into the kitchen. You won't last long here. I'm a winner. One more win and I'll be a pro. One more win! Just watch me!"

The man beside me on the bleachers snickered. "That's old Ernie. He's been threatening to turn pro for as long as I've known him. And that's a while."

"How do you turn pro?" I honestly wanted to know. "Is there money to be made in shuffleboard?"

"Lord, no! The way it goes is, you make your money and *then* you play shuffleboard. A pro means you have won so many amateur tournaments it's not fair for you to compete with the beginners any more. That's all." He grinned. "We better stop talking. Has to be absolutely quiet around here."

"You mean the contestants aren't allowed to talk to each other?"

"Not during tournament play. They can talk to the officials if they need to ask about the lie of one of the shots, but not to each other. You can tell a real greenhorn because he starts running up and down the court yelling about what disk is on the line, or what counts. Bad."

All the time we had been talking, Ruth had been carefully lining up her yellow disks and had managed to out-shoot and out-play old Ernie mercilessly. That meant good news and bad news. She had won that match, but she had to play another winner, and so on. Meanwhile, Howard had entered the Sisters in doubles with Bess as their fourth, and they were causing quite a stir.

"Come watch these nuns!" people behind me were saying. I thought of Yellowstone and the betting. I called to Wentworth.

"Jim, you don't see any signs of trouble, do you?"

"Like maybe a fiver changing hands in the gallery? No. This crowd is too by-the-rules for that."

And by-the-rules they were. It took until almost eleven o'clock for Ruth to lose and shake herself loose from more play. Emmett had drawn a bye to begin with and wound up second in something. His trophy was about five inches high, but he tickled all of us by being so proud. Good for Emmett.

As for our "girls' team," we could all be proud. Those ladies swept the field, but just then the photographers from the local papers showed up, followed by a television news team. Howard blew his whistle and we high-tailed it for our bus, leaving the other participants and the officials standing there staring.

"See you folks in Bakersfield!" Howard shouted over the roar of the motor as George beat a hasty retreat — just in time.

George won "last driver." Only Sister Anne and I had not piloted that grand coach at one time or another along the way. Even Katherine had driven. She lasted about three miles but thanked George profusely for the privilege. Now, for the last leg of our journey George had won the toss, so to speak. He could run that baby all the way to Redlands or he could pass the baton whenever he chose. I really think Lorraine rigged the whole affair, but nobody minded at all.

Just west of Phoenix, at Buckeye, George picked up the microphone.

"Ruth, can you hear me?" Ruth waved. "One more fuel stop here? We have a big desert ahead."

"Fine, George. We have enough to 'fillerup' once more. Won't take all that to get us home, but we can leave some for Trailways. That seems fair. She was half full when we . . . adopted . . . her."

Ruth laughed. "You know," she said to nobody in particular, "we're basically nice people."

Jim laughed, too. "Well, don't sound so surprised! Why do you think I chose your table for bingo years ago? You are basically nice people! All of you!"

I wanted to say, "All of us, Jim." But I didn't.

George pulled into a dinky truck stop the other side of Buckeye. Saturday afternoon quiet. "These guys must have been goofy putting this pump so close to the wall that only one vehicle can be serviced at a time. Old station, you can tell."

Even I could tell that much. The place must have been the original Buckeye Truck Stop. Probably in the back somewhere we could find the old sign, "EAT HERE GET GAS," we used to think was so funny. They probably sold cactus candy in what was now a grimy scrunched-up office furnished with one showcase with a cracked glass top and two boxes of Hershey bars. Even the cash register and the phone looked too greasy to touch. I had gone in to ask for the key to the ladies' room, but I climbed right back on the bus.

George and Ruth had their routine about paying and all the rest of the conversation down pat. They had answered the same questions so many times all of us knew their answers. I guess Ruth had acquired that facility from being married to Emmett, since they had no children. I had thought only mothers had that many standard answers.

Back in the driver's seat, George remarked casually, "I'll have to back her up to get out of here. This surely is a stupid arrangement of these pumps."

The engine gave a satisfying roar and George shifted gears. Nothing happened. He jiggled the handle, waggled the gearshift in neutral, and tried again. Nothing. He tried other gears besides reverse. Still frozen right there. There was a grinding noise but no response to get us going backwards.

I had the bad luck to be sitting right next to Emmett. He looked straight at me, then beyond me to Ruth.

"What did I tell you, Ruth? From the very first minute I said this was a crazy, juvenile thing to do! But no, you had to drag along with all these kooks! Now we're still almost three hundred miles from home and this old bus has broken down! Just like when Captain Nice up here found it! What shall we do now, Ruth? Take a bus to Palm Springs?"

"Feel free, Emmett." I'm sorry, but I couldn't help saying it. Ruth was still holding the shuffleboard trophy. She grinned.

George opened the door and headed for the greasy garage, where three men were leaning against the workbench, staring at a partially dismantled pickup truck.

"You have a mechanic on duty?"

The men stared at George as if he were a part of the pickup.

"Are any of you guys mechanics?" I saw them shaking their heads. Then Howard went out to stand behind George and Jim went, then Emmett. That left the women on board the wagons, waiting to be rescued by the cavalry. George was waving his hands in the air, gesturing about some tool or something, I suppose. Finally, the oldest man came out of the garage and stood where we could see him. And hear him. If there's anything can turn a bunch of women into frenzied rabbits, it's not being able to hear what's going on.

"You won't get a mechanic here at five-thirty on a Saturday afternoon, mister. Not even if you've got a gold Triple-A card. I'd say you're fresh outa' luck."

"Now, just one minute, here! Surely there's someone in this town who knows something about repairs! If I can't get this coach in reverse I can't pull away from that pump and you can't sell any more gas. You might miss a lot of business!"

One of the younger men ambled out to join the crowd. "Close in thirty minutes anyway."

The third man had been lounging in the background, chewing on a toothpick. He faced George and Howard now. Howard took over. "Now, look here! We've got to get this bus out of here and down the road. We have a big tournament in Blythe first thing in the morning.

I'm the coach of this team, and I need these people well rested and ready. We're tied for second in the league. I mean, we're not talking just tourists here! We have to be there or we'll forfeit and there goes second place!"

Howard snapped his fingers, to emphasize the importance of the moment, I suppose.

"Now, we are not the first vehicle in fifty years to have trouble shifting gears in this town," he said carefully. "Right? Somebody around here knows how to deal with such problems. Right? You just tell us who that might be, and we'll talk to him about moving us on out of here. Okay? If we don't make it to Blythe tonight —"

"Well," the middle man spoke, "Purd is the best mechanic around, but he won't take no jobs on motors or anything on Saturday or Sunday. He's a good mechanic, but he's also the preacher at the Born Again Church of Faith and Healing, up the road. On Saturday he works on preparing his message. You can't get Purd to look at any kind of a engine 'til Monday morning. And then he's usually wore out from all that preachin'."

For some reason, Howard had perked up a lot. "Purd?" he said. "Purd? By any chance are you referring to Purd Manire? He used to be the best mechanic I ever saw, but it's been several years. Not many around named Purd, though." He laughed and slapped his knee. "You mean Purd Manire?"

Suddenly the men were friendlier. I'd had visions of being run out of town on a rail if we angered this trio. Or hunted down by a posse.

"Sure! Purd Manire! But he won't do any work today. You'll have to wait 'til —"

"What's his number? How can I reach old Purd?" Howard again. Our other men stood speechless.

"No need for a phone, mister. Purd lives right there in that white house. He owns this place. He's there right now. His truck's there. But he's working on his —"

"We'll *see* what he's working on," Howard said politely.

One knock at the door brought out a tall, skinny man wearing bleached old overalls and a Pennzoil cap. Howard stood stock still.

"Sir, we have a problem with this bus over here," he said in this funny voice. "Won't go into reverse so we can't pull away from your pump there. We already paid a helluva lot of money for the gas. Now we need to get on to Blythe before morning."

He stopped and waited expectantly. "Well?"

"Brother, I sure am sorry to hear about your problem, but I have to work on my message for the services tomorrow. I'll be more than happy to take a look at your bus on Monday. If they've got all the parts I can generally make 'em run. But right now —"

"Hear that, guys?" Howard was crowing. "I heard this honyok say that a hundred times! 'If they got all the parts I can generally make 'em run.' That's what you always said back in the old days, didn't you, Purd?"

Purd Manire stepped off his miniscule porch and shaded his eyes with his hand. "Who —? Who —? Have I seen you somewhere before, mister?"

"Just all over Kansas and Missouri and Iowa and Oklahoma and — come on, Purd!" Howard stuck out his hand. "Howard Lanning! Remember? Remember that twelve-cylinder Packard we hauled booze in from the Canadian border to — you and I, Purd. And Shorty Kibler and Red Snyder. Those were the good old days!"

Howard turned to his astonished friends. "You talk about life in the fast lane, these three guys and I worked for — well, never mind, but we had one fine time in the old days! Wouldn't you say so, Purd?"

Purd just made like a statue. Better be a bird, Purd, I thought. Then I was ashamed of myself for such a silly thought.

"Tell you what, Purd. My team and I can forfeit. We can pick up master points on the shuffleboard circuit anytime. I'd like to stay right here 'til Monday because I don't want anyone but you to touch this vehicle. We got a huge investment. I don't trust any other mechanic like I would you, Purd. So what do you say? We'll just stay right here and enjoy Buckeye for the weekend. I'd sure like to come to your church, Purd! Yeah. I'd sure like to do that! Then maybe when you ask for witnesses and all that, I can give a real testimonial about how we used to live and now you've seen the light and how much I admire what you're doing here!"

Howard had to speak up for the last part of that recitation as he followed Purd over to the bus. In less than half an hour we were back on the road.

Emmett hadn't said one word the whole time.

❧

The port of entry at Blythe always shines in the night like an island of brightness in such a blank space. As usual, there were a couple of cars ahead of us, even after midnight, and a couple of trucks on the other side. George stepped out on the platform while Wentworth carried off the routine with the papers.

Howard and Lorraine and I stood on the platform, too, stretching out the kinks. It had been a long day. George sauntered over to talk with Howard.

I just looked at that sentence. Four or five weeks ago I could never have said that George "sauntered" anywhere. What a change hath been wrought here! Bless Bess!

"Howard, I can't tell you how much fun it was to watch Purd's expression as he realized who you were. It must be fun to run into people you've met before. I never run into anyone. I guess all the folks I knew riding my line back in Pennsylvania are still riding those same routes. I'll have to go back there again to see anyone I've ever seen before."

"Well, we certainly loved seeing all those old friends of yours up there, George. They'd be worth another trip any time."

I had said this trying to be polite more than anything, but George suddenly had a strange look on his face. He was watching a man over in the truck lanes. This tall, dark young man stood beside a Yellow Freight Lines truck — a big semi. He had an open-neck shirt and a black driver's cap perched on the back of his head.

George was staring at the kid, who seemed to recognize George. The kid didn't pay any attention to the rest of us but walked straight over to George.

"Hi! How'ya been?"

"Oh . . . fine, thanks."

The younger man turned his attention to our coach. "Golden Roamers Shuffleboard Team? Florida? Funny, mister, I was sure I'd seen you someplace, but I've never been to Florida."

"Maybe I just resemble somebody you know," George said, sort of sullen, I thought. Then he turned away and climbed back on the bus. He had the motor started before the rest of us were half-way aboard.

Bess had watched the whole scene. "George, you're not going to make friends running into people if you just turn your back! That young man seemed interested in you. And you say you never run into people you've known someplace else?"

George had the bus back into traffic before he answered Bess.

"That young man was the whippersnapper who abandoned me — and this coach! Do you think I'm about to let him put two and two together while he talks about how he's never been to Florida?"

Bess did what she thought was best under the circumstances. She raised her arms in cheerleader fashion and led us in one rousing chorus of George's song:

> *For I want to hire out as the Skipper*
> *Who dodges life's stress and life's strains;*
> *Of the trolley, the Toonerville trolley,*
> *The trolley that meets all the trains.*

The rest of the trip was absolute peace. We rolled into the driveway of the Queen of Missions to find Jake waiting there. Reluctantly, we all claimed our luggage from the compartments and cleared out the boxes, books, tapes, word-processor, and playing cards.

Bess broke the silence. "There's not much to say, friends, except thanks.

"It's been just wonderful." Ruth stood next to Emmett, her arms loaded with stuff.

"You're right, Ruth, this has been wonderful," Emmett said.

George put his arm around Gladys, and sighed. "One thing I'd like to ask, Sister, but I'm not sure of the right way to say this. Would you, Sister Anne, as they say, dismiss us?"

Sister Anne smiled and bowed her head. We all bowed our heads, too.

"Thank you, blessed Lord, for the gift of friendship and the warmth of the love of caring people. And thank you very much for the use of this beloved bus."

I couldn't help adding, "George and Bess, you know how we all feel about this adventure. We shall be forever grateful. Now, let's get started on Operation: Rescue Mission and get on with our lives!"

Jim Wentworth put his arm around my shoulders. He looked me right in the eye. "Yes, Lillian. Let's get on with our lives."

"Let's!"

Bless Bess!

⮧

WHAT DIFFERENCE DOES IT MAKE?

D on't ask me who had the best time on our impromptu tour. Here I sit at my own desk on Sunday morning. Bags still parked in the entryway where Jim left them. Nothing for breakfast in the refrigerator. No Sunday *Times* on the front step. None of my orderly life in order. And I don't care. Right now, I want to think back on these past weeks.

The only thing I have unpacked is my journal. Bright and early this morning I dug the pages out of the carrying case and propped myself on my own pillows. Not that I read every word. That will come later. Today I wanted an overview of what worked and what didn't. How did our expectations still trapped here in my little home in Snug Harbor compare with the reality of our journey? After just a few minutes of reliving these days, I had to jump out of bed and set up my Toshiba for one more go-round. Before I forgot my astute observations.

This machine and I have become so accustomed to each other, it's almost automatic. Sometimes I look at what appears on the screen and wonder, "Now, how did this little wizard know that?" Seems I almost write it before I think it. Should I worry about that?

All along the way we have all been aware of a changing atmosphere on our bus. Bess mentioned it before we ever got out of California. "Did you notice how much George smiles?" she'd say. Or, "Howard never was this friendly back at the dock." I didn't tell her, but she is friendlier and more relaxed herself. Not just our attitudes changed. We started calling each other by our first names — even Sister Anne did that. And the dress code gradually shifted from our classic prints and matching sweaters and dress slacks and sport shirts to bus-oriented apparel like souvenir T-shirts and Bermuda shorts. Everybody arrived back at Snug Harbor with new sneakers.

Now it will be interesting to see what else has changed.

My doorbell just rang. Change number one.

❧

Journal? Who has time to keep a journal? Today is Thursday and I haven't had time to sit at this machine since Jim rang my bell before nine on Sunday morning. I haven't had such a hug in years. We greeted each other as if we hadn't seen one another for eight years, instead of eight hours.

"How about breakfast at the Mess?"

"Why not? There's certainly nothing in this place worth eating. Besides, I was already missing the Roamers. We can't break off our groupie life cold turkey now, can we?"

Thus began Phase Two. We strolled over to the Captain's Mess in time to join most of the others. All except Emmett and Ruth. No way would she get out of baking his biscuits after three weeks. But I'll bet he ate them with a smile.

The energy apparent in our crowd amazes me. Before Sunday ended, we had introduced Gladys to most of Snug Harbor. She's staying in the Guest Quarters until next week, when she and George will be married. I'll admit, we've generated some quizzical looks from neighbors, who probably didn't realize we'd been away until we got back. Now they seem glad to see us. Want to stop and visit about where we've been. I just answer, "visiting friends."

My kids are most pleased about my trip, from the little I've told them. They never even ask about the bus. They seem to think I flew all these places on my own with my friends like a flock of Mary Poppinses. They don't care, I don't mind. When I do talk to one or the other the consensus is they're happy I have such nice friends, and who's this Jim person?

Now, about the others and the Project.

Since Monday, Emmett and Sister Helen Eugene have resurrected every garden tool known to man or beast from the sheds and barns at the mission. In three days the place looks better. The shuffleboard court is in working order already. Old Mike's amazement equals Sister Anne's enthusiasm. Even the cats seem overjoyed.

Bess spent many hours during the ride from the Mother House to Snug Harbor in intense conversation with Sister Frances Jo Ann, who seems to know the most about working with youngsters and keeping a mission in operation. Actually, they had clipboards and notebooks filled with plans before we ever disembarked from our glorious chariot. Instead of our usual Girls' Day Out on Tuesday, Bess went with Sister Frances Jo Ann for an appointment with juvenile authorities of some sort at the court house in San Bernardino. Sister Anne scurried all over Redlands spreading the news. She and Jim Wentworth cornered a banker first thing Monday morning to set all sorts of wheels turning.

Ruth and Katherine and I are looking into the possibilities of opening up the rest of the mansion. Katherine wants to start a library, which is most logical. The shelves are already there in a beautiful paneled room. Dancing about that musty place planning her part of the project, Katherine is Noel Coward's *Blithe Spirit* personified.

No way can I tell you how busy George is. Whirling dervish. He and Gladys beam at each other. Last night George missed calling "Bingo!" twice because he simply wasn't paying attention to his card. Lorraine brought it to his attention, but somebody else had already won the money.

You wonder why I haven't mentioned the Lannings. Right? Well, we're all so busy during the day we don't see much of them because they have a project of their own. Not only does Howard insist that Lorraine walk his daily circle with him and get into this fitness routine for his heart, they both informed us they will attend the recommended "ninety meetings in ninety days" in AA. For a fleeting moment they considered signing in at Betty Ford's place, but they decided to stay here where we all can and will act as a support group. That will be a tough road, but eventually they'll get into the swing of the mission and that will benefit the sisters as well as their clients.

Now the most important character of this journal: our bus.

Before bingo last night, we Roamers gathered at Bess's to watch the local news. That same young man I like so much read through the more important happenings then signed off with a story that obviously amused him immensely.

"Here's an update, folks, on the Case of the Missing Bus. Remember several weeks ago, Trailways reported they had lost a bus? A forty-six-passenger Landcruiser? They had last seen their big bus on I-10 between Beaumont and Palm Springs. For weeks the company has searched for this vehicle. This afternoon that bus reappeared on that same stretch of Interstate, apparently abandoned.

"But there's more to the story. An anonymous caller reported the location of the bus to the highway patrol and to Trailways about three this afternoon. The bus is in perfect condition, company officials report. Best of all, folks, listen to this: Taped to the steering wheel of that bus was a thank-you note obviously written on a word processor. The note said, 'Your wonderful coach has saved our lives. Thank you.' Now how about that? There's good news tonight, after all."

So even Jake did his part.

❧

End of this journal. I'll start a new one in a day or two. Some about the mission, that's for sure. And maybe about another excursion, or maybe about two people in love.

Why not?

❧

THE GOLDEN ROAMERS' SEARCH FOR . . .
A SHUFFLEBOARD TOURNAMENT?

Keep reading!
Following is an excerpt from
Frances Weaver's other new book

Where Do Grandmothers Come From?
(And Where Do They Go?)

Here's what one reader wrote about this autobiography of a woman who isn't about to let aging slow her down:

Dear Fran:

I have certainly enjoyed "Where Do Grandmothers Come From?" as it could have been written about the town in the Midwest I grew up in, Quincy, Illinois. It brought to mind things I had not considered for 40 or 50 years. Thank you for sharing the book with me, and if you don't mind I would appreciate your autographing it when you are in the bank.

Best regards,

Philip W. Hocker

Vice President and Trust Officer
Pueblo Bank and Trust

7

NOW, ABOUT THOSE GRANDPARENTS . . .

J oe, let's go feed the chickens." With those words, Allison wrapped her Grandfather Weaver around her little finger.

The Weavers kept chickens in their back yard in Concordia, to the delight of our youngsters but the dismay of neighbors sick of crowing roosters. From the time they moved to Republican Street in 1924 Joe and Vesta had kept chickens in town. Vesta had the laying hens. Joe raised game cocks. Don't get me wrong, here, Joe Weaver did not raise fighting chickens; he and Vesta just liked the spectacular plumage of the game cocks and treated them as pets.

One of the big events for little Weavers, ours and their cousins, would be the day Joe brought Hector, King of the Roosters, into the kitchen and held Hector erect on the kitchen scale while Vesta took a picture of the two of them posing for posterity. Knowing Hector's weight from month to month apparently meant a lot. For these photography sessions, Joe needed heavy gloves. Hector objected strenuously to his weigh-ins, squawking and pecking in all directions, which delighted the children even more.

Joe also posed with his home-grown tomatoes on that scale every summer. It didn't take long for the little people of the family to understand that Joe's chickens and his tomatoes were the key to enjoying that wonderful back yard.

Actually, Joe Weaver had a hard time disguising his disappointment when his first grandchild turned out to be a girl, but Allison won him over all by herself as soon as she learned to say "Joe."

Joe had been an athlete, a runner at Kansas University. My sons still have some of Joe's medals from the KU Relays. When I first knew him in the early '40s he was still in pretty good shape, about 5′11″, weighed 175, I'd guess. Later on, his penchant for making and sampling home brew put more of a paunch on him, but Joe never could have been called a big man—not like his sons or like Vesta's family. He kept his curly hair in a crew cut and always wore bow ties. (Now, what made me remember the bow ties after all these years?) Joe Weaver could have been described in many ways, I suppose, but nobody ever referred to him as a "snappy dresser."

Joe had devoted most of his active parenting life to making a fine athlete of his son, John. John's older brother, Joe, Jr., had no interest or ability on the football field or in the swimming pool, but John was a natural and Joe made the most of that. Hour after hour, day after day, year after year, Joe coached John to be a champion swimmer even though the Concordia High School had no swim team and no coach.

When he was not holding the stop watch beside the school pool, Joe sat in the bleachers during every football practice and certainly never missed a game. He never missed telling John how to do it better, either.

Concordia won the League, John won the honors, then John set state records for breast stroke and back stroke which "stood" for many years in the annals of Kansas high-school swimming and the local AAU, for which Joe gave himself full credit. Joe considered himself a man's man.

⁊

During this lifetime I've met some conservative people, but when it comes to outright compulsion for security, Joe Weaver takes the cake. This angle to his personality figured into his grandparenting, so it counts here. Perhaps his negativity stemmed from what we now recognize as mild depression. At any rate, Joe's father and his two older brothers were doctors. Doctor Asa Weaver had his own hospital and a lively practice in Concordia. Brother Ross Weaver practiced radiology at St. Joseph Hospital there. Glenn Weaver lived in west Texas, I believe, where he was a psychiatrist.

The last thing Joe wanted was an M.D. after his name, even

though the family expected that. The tension and constant pressure of KU medical school drove him absolutely crazy. He agonized over every pop quiz and suffered through every lab report. The thought of being responsible for the well-being of patients was more than he could bear.

When Asa Weaver, M.D., died during Joe's second year of medical school, that poor miserable soul beat it home to Concordia as fast as he could get there, settled on a farm the family owned out east of town, married Vesta, and never again thought of being a doctor.

Even the insecurity of farming worked on Joe with his negative attitudes. He hated it when it rained, worried even more when it didn't. Vesta and the rest of the family understood this, so everyone sighed with relief when Joe Weaver went to work for the Post Office.

It is significant to note here that Glenn Weaver, the shrink, brought his wife and young son to live with Joe and Vesta during the Depression when postal clerks were paid but doctors were not. Joe pointed that out regularly.

Being a postal clerk in the days when sorting mail by hand involved knowing every route of every train west of any given point suited Joe. He worked hard at being the best sorter and the most efficient clerk at the window on sunny or cloudy days, with a regular paycheck and Vesta to drive him back and forth to work. He worked 7:00 to 3:00 so he had after-school time for coaching John and, years later, spending time every day with the grandkids when we spent half-summers in Kansas during medical school.

His talent for anticipating the worst of any situation never left Joe. Our youngest son, Matthew, was born when Allison was thirteen, her brothers eight and eleven. All three of the "big kids" absolutely adored their new brother and cared for the baby devotedly.

Joe, whose favorite expression about any child was "poor little soul," would watch this carrying-on about baby Matthew and shake his head sadly.

"It's a shame those bigger kids are so crazy about Matt," he'd say. "If anything happens to that baby and he gets sick and dies, those kids won't be able to take it."

Typical Joe Weaver logic.

Happily, Joe was not around when Matt broke his head. One morning I asked eight-year-old Ross to watch his baby brother, who was lying on the couch. I went to the kitchen for some reason and Matt rolled off, hitting his head on the foot of the coffee table. That poor little head had a dent like an old ping pong ball, so off we went to the doctor, the hospital, surgery, and all the rest. Our darling baby boy came out a cue ball kid. Joe would have wound up on the couch himself.

Months later I realized Ross spent time out in the back yard alone, after dark in that big yard by himself. One evening I questioned him.

"Ross, what are you doing out there in the back yard in the dark all by yourself? It's cold. What's the idea?"

Ross gave me a soft smile. "Mother, I didn't want you to know this, but I've been going to the back yard to pray."

Pray? An eight-year-old meditating in the garden, as they say?

"How lovely, Ross." I smiled at him. "Are you praying about anything in particular?" Christmas was coming.

Again this sappy smile. "Mother, I've been praying to God to forgive me because I let my baby brother fall off the couch and hurt his head so he had to have an operation."

"How thoughtful of you, Ross. You are such a fine big brother," I said as I reached to hug him.

Ross reeked of cigar smoke.

"While you've been praying have you been smoking your dad's cigars out there in the dark by yourself?"

"Oh, no."

"Ross, you smell like cigar smoke. Are you telling me you haven't been smoking?"

"Mother, I have not been smoking. I have been trying to smoke but I can't get 'em lit. So I just tried. I did not smoke."

That story might be beside the point, but it has always been a favorite of mine. Ross is not too fond of my telling it.

∾

I have quizzed my sons and daughter about their memories of their grandparents. Of Joe they have agreed. They recall the rides. Joe and Vesta would pile grandkids into their Ford and take off across country roads for hours, stopping in farming communities along the way for pop or ice cream.

Vesta did the town driving, Joe took the wheel when they headed for the country, but both drove that old Ford as if it had an automatic shift. Once down the alley and onto Republican Street, they shoved that old car into second and never touched the gearshift again until they needed to back up. Cloud County, Kansas, is hilly, green and pleasant along the Republican River. The children collected limestone fossils and Vesta took pictures of kids lined up in front of windmills.

When they grew old enough to visit grandparents by themselves Joe loved taking our boys to his barber. They returned from visits to Kansas with crew cuts that were generally very bad, but they had had a good time with Joe.

One favorite place to visit on their rides was the ramshackle house of Boston Corbett, Concordia's celebrity. Boston Corbett's claim to fame was shooting John Wilkes Booth, after which he (Corbett) was dishonorably discharged and moved to Kansas.

They also explored the country around Glasco, Kansas, where Vesta had grown up. Joe made fun of Vesta, constantly teasing about Glasco, Kansas, in the heart of the Solomon Valley where it's richest and widest and best. Just like some of the small town "humor" we had down around McPherson.

The Weavers lived across the street from the high school, just up the hill from the athletic field. Their yellow frame house with a great front porch typified mid-America without any of the frills or "pretensions" of some of Concordia's wealthier neighborhoods.

Vesta cooked on her old gas stove long after similar models were appearing in museums and antique stores. That seemed to be Vesta's choice. Vesta Cool Weaver made a fetish of not "putting on airs." Taller than Joe by an inch or so, Vesta out-weighed her husband by ten pounds most of her life. She was a sturdy, stocky, sensible woman who wore heavy black oxfords and braided her hair. Her clothes reflected her disdain for any fanciness: one black dress for funerals and church, housedresses, which she usually trimmed with a bit of rick-rack and a front zipper. She knew everyone in town and was universally admired for her kindness and caring for others. Not that Vesta was a saint. She simply cared.

Mostly, however, Vesta cared for Joe. This irritated me early in our marriage. "She lets Joe walk all over her," I'd say. "She waits on him hand and foot, fixing him special salads, driving him to work, shushing the kids so Joe can rest, running all of his errands, putting up the storm windows. She even peels tomatoes for him. She's nuts!" I yelled at John.

He'd always defend her taking all this guff and his reasoning made some sense: Vesta'a mother had died when Vesta and her brother and sister were quite small. They had grown up in a house with their father and their maternal grandmother, so Vesta had no role model of wife-type behavior to follow. She had no real example of marriage, so she assumed Joe was generally right about most everything. She probably thought all wives were indentured to their spouses.

After two years of college, she had married Joe. After a year or so they settled into their idea of marriage: Joe worked at the post office and Vesta worked at everything else. She emphasized simplicity, pragmatism and common sense with the rest of us.

Our memorable meals at Weavers, for Vesta was an excellent cook, invariably are recalled as the times Vesta made hamburgers. Vesta's gravy, pies, fried chicken (fresh from the back yard) and delicious biscuits could not hold a candle to her hamburgers. She cooked and served only four at a time, even for the entire family. Not fat, bulky burgers but skinny burgers in skinny buns. Hot from her stove, each patted fresh and instantly fried. For years I tried to duplicate the magic of Vesta's hamburgers, but never made the grade.

Vesta's cooking far outshone her housekeeping. Her favorite expression, "a man on a galloping horse would never see it," applied to any sort of flaw or oversight in their home. If some more important project like a ride to the country interfered, almost any sort of household chores could wait.

❦

It is important to note here, however, that Joe and Vesta were savers. We'll go into that later, but for now picture a back-porch work bench piled high with old newspapers, rusted tools, jars of nails, skillets without handles and baskets full of holes. The buffet in the dining room could be seen in its original glory only when a death in the family brought everyone to the Weavers and Vesta cleared off the buffet for the company. The walls were covered with pictures of everyone they had ever known because "Joe likes things out where he can see 'em."

I asked Allison, now over forty years old, how she remembers Vesta. Allison's eyes mist when the name is mentioned.

"Vesta could always fix things. Vesta could always make everything all right. I knew when I was little I could depend on Vesta to help me. She made things for me—like that purple square-dance skirt and doll clothes. She sang in the car or whistled. Sometimes she'd just pat my hand."

The boys felt the same way. Whatever needed doing, Vesta could do it. They undoubtedly got that message from Joe. And generally they were right. Vesta could fix almost anything. Some of the extension cords draped around the dining room caused some of us to shudder, but Vesta made almost everything work.

Until John's graduation from medical school in Philadelphia, when my dad loaned his new station wagon to the Weavers to drive east for the big event and help us move our meager belongings westward, Vesta had never been out of Kansas. Her father, a most successful farmer and banker, had taken his son to market in Kansas City, but his girls stayed right on the farm where he knew they belonged. He also left his farm to the men of the family, not the women. Typical of the attitudes of the day, I'd assume, but outrageous by today's standards.

In spite of her truly provincial upbringing and her incomplete college education, Vesta Weaver had one of the keenest minds I have ever known. Her inquisitiveness, her interest in the world around her, her obsession with words and their derivation, made her good company from the first day we met. These qualities she imparted to her grandchildren. Vesta seldom left a question unanswered. She and the kids would look it up, whether something from conversation or a book or a Scrabble game. The more I write about her, the more I realize how much I admired Vesta. We were good friends.

ი

My own parents resembled the Weavers only in being Kansans. Joe and my father could not have been more different. Joe was friendly enough, certainly, but John Allison greeted everyone he met as a long-lost buddy, telling funny stories or making comic observations to the delight of anyone around. Dad also lived by taking risks, by inventing and promoting all sorts of schemes, which sometimes worked but which sometimes went right back to the drawing board or into the trash.

Some said John Allison and John Weaver looked enough alike to be father and son. I never agreed, but the two of them did have a lot in common and enjoyed throughout their lives a special bond. Both weighed well over two hundred pounds on a yo-yo sliding scale. Both were barrel-chested and had slim hips so their trousers were always at half mast. Dad had wavy thick hair that had been red in his youth. John was more of a blonde. They died less than three years apart, and both left all of us with some very funny and some rather painful stories. But that had little to do with the grandparent part that concerns our children and my parents at this point.

The lifestyle of my parents contrasted with that of John's folks from the beginning. My folks were always traveling, and business kept my father on the road when Mother was at home. The money was different, certainly, and that made one of the big contrasts in their grandparenting.

Basically, John's parents "did" for our children while my parents "bought" for them. That meant a lot for us as parents to appreciate on both sides. Our children's winter coats and other major wardrobe items were paid for by my mother while John trained for surgery at resident's starvation wages. Once in a while my dad would drop off an extra car for us to use, or they would offer us "extra" furniture, or Dad brought John some of his expensive clothes he claimed he'd tired of wearing. My parents paid for my cleaning help in Kansas City.

ɔ

Looking back, I am relatively certain there were chickens at my folks's house, too, but they lived on a splendid ranch north of Colorado Springs where the gardener tended the tomatoes and the farmer's wife brought in the eggs. Nobody weighed the roosters in the kitchen like Joe did in Concordia. Foothill Farms certainly did not resemble Republican Street in any way. There were ponies, a swimming pool, lakes stocked with trout and teeming with bluegills, a guest house, and a big house filled with treasures not to be touched by little hands. All with Pikes Peak as a backdrop.

Allison and Chris were the first grandchildren on either side of the family. They paved the way for the rest of the grandchildren, including two more of our own. Ross was born in Kansas City, Matthew after we moved to Colorado.

Moving to Colorado brought much closer extended-family contacts, since by that time all of my sisters and my parents lived in Pueblo and Colorado Springs. The Colorado grandparents who occasionally had been a part of our children's lives now lived just up the road. Joe and Vesta Weaver were farther away than ever, therefore more fun to visit for longer vacations without John and me.

My mother, Marn Allison, turned out to be an entirely different kind of a grandmother than Vesta or my own Grandmother Allison. She is, after all, an entirely different kind of a person. Her primary concern has been orderliness. My mother keeps things neat. She prefers her environment quiet and her surroundings undisturbed. That means our children have probably driven her to distraction and her responses have been predictable: She has enjoyed her grandchildren less because they annoyed her just by being kids. To say that this has resulted in stress on both sides would be the understatement of the year.

I feel safe in saying that my mother's greatest joy as a grandmother came from being with "the little girls." Our youngest sister Mary and her family lived on the ranch with Mother and Dad when their three daughters were little girls. They were three of the prettiest, cutest, brightest youngsters I have known, and Mother truly enjoyed having them around. The little girls traveled with Grammy and Grampy. The little girls were model grandkids.

Most of all, the little girls were not little boys.

Two stories about my son Chris come to mind. Just able to walk around and explore at Grammy's house, Chris headed for the forbidden coffee table and lifted the lid of an antique glass butter dish, one of Grammy's Things. Mother yelled at him, "put that down, Chris!" so startling him that he slammed the lid back on, smashing it into a thousand pieces and breaking both his and Grammy's hearts.

Chris's heart was certainly not broken years later when we took Mother with us to watch Chris in his first football game. The bleachers were small, right behind the bench. Mother watched Chris going in and out of the game as long as she could stand it. Then she called shrilly, "Chris! Chris! Pull up your socks, honey!" The look on that 16-year-old tackle's face broke my heart.

We need to remember that my mother apparently had never had much of a relationship with her own grandparents, therefore no role model or pattern to follow. Her own mother died before we girls spent time in that household. So Mother never saw her own mother as a grandmother.

Where do grandmothers come from? From the beginnings of our lives, that's where.

Besides that, during our growing up years Mother had to be the stabilizing influence, the Rock of Gibraltar, while her husband dashed around the country in one business venture and then another. We girls must have been four burdens to Mom, who has never been an extrovert in any sense of the word. She guarded us with her life. Dad turned out to be a great provider, but it was Mother who kept the family and the finances on an even keel. When grandchildren came along, Mother did the best she could in providing for our needs as mothers, but sitting on the floor playing cars with little boys simply was not her cup of tea. It has taken most of our family a long, long time to figure that one out.

Now she needs us as she never expected to, and the indignity of such dependence makes life even harder for all of us. Many families face such trauma these days. We just need to cope with aged grand-mothers as we wished they would cater to our children. It's a matter of taking turns.

&